Windows II

A book for those with a heart for helping kids heal

24 illuminating stories for helping youngsters understand
and deal with the impact of crisis, loss ... and life

by Dr. James D. Sutton

Friendly Oaks Publications

Pleasanton, Texas

Windows II

A book for those with a heart for helping kids heal

by Dr. James D. Sutton

———————————————

published by:
Friendly Oaks Publications
PO Box 662
Pleasanton, TX 78064
830.569.3586
fax: 830.281.2617
e-mail: friendly@DocSpeak.com

Library of Congress Cataloging-in-Publication Data

Sutton, James D.
    Windows II : a book for those with a heart for helping kids heal / by James D. Sutton.
        p. cm.
    Includes bibliographical references.
    ISBN 1-878878-60-3 (pbk.)
        1. Interpersonal conflict in children--Study and teaching (Elementary) 2. Interpersonal conflict in adolescence--Study and teaching (Secondary) 3. Problem solving in children--Study and teaching (Elementary) I. Title: Windows 2. II. Title: Windows two. III. Title.

BF723.I645 S88 2002
155.9'071--dc21

                                                                2001040855

International Standard Book Number: 1-878878-60-3
$21.50 (US)

Table of Contents

Foreword

As a veteran crisis counselor, I've long believed we should be proactive in training individuals who help traumatized children recover. But in my work with parents and child service professionals, I found so few creative materials that addressed a caregiver's specific needs in assisting these youngsters.

I had used Dr. James Sutton's work, widely known and utilized in the field; his sensitivity on the subject is unparalleled. So I called him. Jim was patient and very helpful in guiding me toward creating *Westwind Publications* in 1997. With his encouragement, I wrote two crisis intervention books in two years. And, as my work continues, I am convinced we need books like this one, *Windows II*.

I believe that children and adolescents in crisis, or those experiencing trauma, can benefit greatly in their recovery by exploring therapeutic stories through discussion and sharing. In doing so, youngsters can gain a clearer understanding of their own situation and how to handle it. The same process also helps siblings and peers achieve clarity with what is happening. Teaching by metaphor and analogy is a strong approach; it offers insights I've grown to count on in crisis counseling.

Windows II provides caregivers with a crafted array of inspirational, educational and highly relevant stories that address the most common issues of recovery from crisis, loss and other traumatic life events. Dr. Sutton's work effectively addresses topics like abuse, anger, perceptions, asking for help, beliefs, hope and points of genuine character.

These poignant stories offer struggling youths new "thinking pathways" of understanding, pathways that illuminate a critical fact: they are *not* alone. Dr. Sutton has added a quick reference for accessing topics, and he provides helpful answers for the discussion elements at the end of each story. But he also encourages caregivers to let youngsters share *their* answers (from *their* experiences) to the questions and activities.

Windows II provides 24 targeted stories that powerfully illustrate issues appearing in crisis situations. It is a wonderful, must-have resource for counselors, teachers, parents and others who have the opportunity and responsibility to help young people heal.

Max A. Swafford, M.Ed.
Crisis consultant and author
The Crisis Manual and *Children in Crisis: A Parents' Guide*
Westwind Publications (www.CrisisInfo.com)

Introduction

A Pleasure (and a Challenge)

A Difficult Work

This book has been both a pleasure and a challenge to put together. It was, without question, the most difficult single work I have ever written. There are a couple of reasons why. First, it addresses issues of human conflict. It's difficult for anyone to effectively address painful issues without getting uncomfortably close to them. Although this might have been productive in the long run, it was not always enjoyable or expedient.

The second reason grew out of the first. I shared much more of myself in this work than in the earlier *Windows* (Friendly Oaks Publications, 1991). When it was a story or an anecdote I had personally experienced, I shared it as such (many of you will recognize that some of these stories have appeared in my newsletter, *Reaching Out)*. If the story happened to me, I stated it as such. I believe we all share best from what we have personally experienced. When we do this well, the incident becomes more than our story; it becomes part of our testimony to life.

Major Overhaul (and then some!)

Many will recall that the first edition of *Windows* was small, containing only seven sections. Yet, it proved to be unique in scope and intent. It was offered as a resource for helping individuals who operate primarily on just two emotions: anger and fear. The first *Windows* focused on the high cost of minimizing and denying of suffering, noting that efforts to "cover it up" are eventually displayed in inappropriate behavior and cumulative misery and illness.

It's bad enough for adults to experience this kind of conflict. It's a tragedy when it happens to a young person.

It pleased me that the earlier version of *Windows* has been a valuable resource for youngsters in a variety of settings—literally from the classroom to the psychiatric hospital. I even know of an instances where the book was used with adults in treatment for drug and alcohol addiction. It was a valuable tool in helping patients positively reconnect with their childhood. Many of them are doing well in their recovery today. Results like these encouraged me to keep plowing through this revision (especially when I didn't feel like it).

Actually, this edition is more like a major overhaul rather than a revision. It has more than three times the stories, questions and activities of the earlier version. (Even then, the majority of these 24 stories actually contain other embedded stories that can be used with or without the other material.) Stories, richly painted with pictures, symbols and emotion, are often the perfect vehicle for presenting an idea or concept in the most revealing, inspiring and unique fashion. They help move a child from confusion to understanding by therapeutically addressing three needs: "language lanes," relief from "terminal uniqueness" and a need for corporate support.

"Language Lanes"

What we're talking about here is the building of avenues to help youngsters expand their emotional bandwidth. When bandwidth opens, inappropriate behavior is reduced.

The concept of bandwidth has been around for some time, but it has taken on a new life because of the Internet. Consumers are shoving more and more e-mail, audio and video down that copper thread we call the phone line. A bandwidth problem develops as the task becomes increasingly time-consuming and frustrating. It's much like trying to route Houston's rush-hour traffic down a cow trail. It could take a week to get through (maybe forever), not to mention the accidents, blown tires and blown tempers along the way.

Some youngsters are trying to emote on considerably less than a copper thread. With no way to move or navigate, it's only a matter of time until their frustration overheats into trouble. Emotional bandwidth is broadened by installing "language lanes" to handle the traffic. Language interfaces with raw emotion so that a youngster can "move" without running everyone off the road. *Windows II* is a collection of tools and material for building "language lanes" that encourage youngsters to write or talk through their concerns rather than to act them out inappropriately.

Relief from "Terminal Uniqueness"

Trouble confuses a youngster, especially when there is no history for dealing with it. Consequently, they not only don't have a way for dealing with the difficulty, they sense it has set up permanent residence. They often feel doomed, that there is no way to deal their situation and that they are the *only* person to have experienced it. They feel "terminally" unique.

Although older children are, by history and experience, better equipped to handle trouble, they can also have difficulty when confronted with an especially powerful or unique challenge. They are likely to feel that their situation is one-of-a-kind, that nothing will *ever* fix it.

Years ago, I worked with a 13-year-old girl who lost both parents in an automobile accident. She fell completely apart (which is pretty understandable). Attempts at living with relatives did not work out, so she was placed in an emergency shelter. One of the child care workers in the shelter brought me something the girl had written. This piece was titled, "Alone":

I'm all alone.

And I rock myself with my arms around me,

Thinking someone loves me.

But deep down inside, I know it's nobody.

I watch everyone being loved but me.

As I look for someone who loves me, I get hurt.

The pain I've been through, I can't forget.

I feel it so strongly that I wish I can forget it all.

But, as I know, I'm all alone,

With nobody at my side.

Alone.

In a few sentences this girl had stated and restated her "terminal uniqueness" with 21 references to self ("I," "myself," "my," and "me"). Even though there were plenty of adults and peers around trying to reach out to her, she was not receptive. Wouldn't it be so easy to become angry at this girl for rejecting our attempts to help her? If you said, "Yes," welcome to the human race. It helps me to keep in mind that, if she knew *exactly* what she should do to be happier and for her life to work out, she would have done it a long time ago.

When we help a youngster break through their "terminal uniqueness," we move them a step closer to resiliency and recovery (not always an easy task). This book is but one tool for helping kids break away from a potentially devastating condition—their own thinking.

A Need for Corporate Support

Obviously the best way for a youngster to deal with "terminal uniqueness" is to realize they are not all that unique at all. The realization that they're not alone in their pain is powerful medicine in and of itself (and a reason why I believe so strongly in group work).

This can be a tough order to fill. Assistance and support from others (especially peers) who have "been there; done that" can be of tremendous benefit. This book is about corporate support.

Using This Book

Each section in this book, with its accompanying stories and ideas, addresses some particular emotional or behavioral issue that might challenge a youngster. Teachers and counselors are urged to use these stories to generate sensitivity about the issue (awareness), to assist youngsters in "buying" the fact that they might be dealing with a shared problem or feeling (corporate support), and to offer some strategies and activities for dealing with the problem or issue being discussed (empowerment).

The last six stories are grouped around a theme of awareness and recovery from compulsive behaviors and disorders. (*The Carpet in My Parlor* is actually about a victim of such behavior, but the questions and activities touch on a common experience of keeping secrets.) Folks familiar with a *Twelve Step* approach to treatment will readily recognize the content.

Questions and activities at the end of each section are intended as guidelines for getting the group going. Because every group is different, discussion often takes on a mind and an agenda of its own. That's great! Be certain to jot down any new ideas that surface; they become excellent material for future questions and activities.

For those folks using this resource in group counseling settings, these stories can make great "starters," either in initially setting up the sessions or as a way to encourage those who might be nervous or reticent to share.

A final thought. As the last parts of this book were being assembled and edited, many individuals lost their lives in the airline hijacking incidents of September 11, 2001. There are losses that cannot be replaced, only healed. As individuals and as a country, however, we will recover. And we shall become even stronger.

JDS

Pleasanton, Texas, 2002

References:

Sutton, J., *Windows*. Pleasanton, TX: Friendly Oaks Publications, 1991 (Out of print).

"Alone" is from the book, *It Makes a Difference*, by James Sutton (Pleasanton, TX: Friendly Oaks Publications, 1990). Reprinted here with permission.

Topic: Handling anger and frustration

You Don't Hit a Killer Whale

Application

This story helps explain how inappropriately expressed anger can send one to the bottom of the pool. The aim of this lesson is to help youngsters develop enough insight into their anger to not only realize its potentially destructive qualities, but how the energy of positive anger can be directed into more appropriate avenues of expression.

Prologue

I'll never forget listening to Terry Kellogg talk about how anger is good. (Terry is an addiction specialist from Minnesota. He was interviewed by John Bradshaw on *The Family* series. These programs received a lot of play on PBS a few years back.)

That's right—anger is *good*. Kellogg noted that anger is our guide to wisdom, and that it provides both energy and direction. Although there's little argument about the energy of anger, its direction, like a rocket, can be directed toward a solution, or go veering dangerously out of control. Either way, it's going somewhere.

The "Red-eye" to Dallas

Let me illustrate with a story that shows both sides. A few years back, I was trying to get home from Pasco, Washington. It was to be a short hop to Salt Lake City, then a straight shot home to San Antonio. When I checked in, I discovered that the flight to Salt Lake had been canceled; I was rerouted through Seattle.

The only flight out of Seattle was a red-eye connecting through Dallas. Of course I wasn't happy about flying all night to get home (a trip made longer by the two time zones crossed), but the guy in front of me at the Delta ticket counter was UPSET! He swore at the ticket agent, ranted

11

and raved, and threatened to shut down the airline. But, when it was all over, he was *still* on the red-eye to Dallas.

Truth is, I have always been fortunate in catching flights, so this delay in getting home was only an inconvenience. It was not a coronary event. Besides, I had packed a great book into my carry-on.

"I have a deal for you," I said as I handed my tickets to the agent. Although he had not fully recovered from the pasting he had taken, I sensed I *did* have his attention.

"Listen," I said, "if you'll get me home the best and quickest way you can, you won't have any trouble from me."

He smiled and nodded, then spent the better part of 15 minutes trying every way possible to fly me home that evening.

As it worked out, I was also on the red-eye to Dallas, but with one big difference. As the agent checked my tickets, he removed a $10.00 meal voucher that had been given to me in Pasco.

"I *can* help you here," he said. He cut me another voucher and handed it to me with my tickets. "I appreciate your patience and understanding. Now this new voucher will get you a steak dinner at the Cuttery Restaurant here in the airport. It's as nice a sit-down place as any you'll find around here."

And it was. I sat near the fireplace and feasted on ribeye and all the trimmings. I finished it off with some great coffee as I read my book and waited for my flight. All for free.

Somewhere in that airport, however, was a guy on my same flight. He was probably eating a quick food taco, complaining about the price, or that the hot sauce was too hot ... or not hot enough.

Frustration is real, but even a halfway decent attitude can turn a taco into a steak.

Following this theme, here's a story about a whale and a whale trainer. Only this time, it was the student who did the teaching.

The Story (*You Don't Hit a Killer Whale*)

A teacher friend of mine shared a story about how a little frustration almost ended in disaster. A friend of his trained killer whales for a popular aquatic theme park. The trainer, wearing the usual scuba gear, was working in the tank one day with one of the whales. On this day (as sometimes happens), the whale was not receptive to the trainer's commands. He tried repeatedly to get the animal to follow his directives.

Frustrated, the trainer hit the whale in the mouth with his fist.

In an instant, the whale worked around behind the trainer and bit down on the scuba tank. He took the trainer down into the water and began spinning him around in a circle. It was all the dizzy and frightened trainer could do to keep the air regulator in his mouth.

The whale stopped and turned him loose. But before the trainer could maneuver away safely, the whale got between him and the surface. The trainer was pinned against the belly of the whale as the animal settled to the bottom of the tank.

The trainer was trapped. Below him was the cement floor; above him was almost 5 tons of whale. But he still had his air supply on his back, and it was working perfectly. He collected his thoughts, relaxed a bit, and figured to just wait it out.

But the whale had the same plan. The inevitable happened; the air supply ran out.

"It was all over," the trainer later shared with my friend. "I was going to drown. I did a stupid thing, and I was going to pay for it with my life."

But at the last instant, the last gasp—we could say—the whale moved away and let him swim to the surface. "I'll let you go," it seemed the animal said to the trainer, "but don't ever hit me like that again."

I'm betting he never did.

Questions/Activities

1. In this story both the trainer and the whale showed that they were upset. Which one, the trainer or the whale, handled their anger the best?

Answer: Probably the whale. Even though he frightened the trainer, he was in control of his behavior at all times. The trainer's behavior was not very well controlled at the moment he hit the whale.

2. Did the whale really want to hurt the trainer? How do you know?

Answer: Of course not. If he had wanted to hurt the trainer he could have killed him instantly with one powerful bite. By the way, the Killer Whale got its name from the fact that they have been observed killing other whales three times their size. They were first called "Whale Killers," but the name got turned around. These whales, sometimes called Orca whales, are by nature friendly toward man. They are in the same family of mammals as the porpoise.

3. It could be said that the whale showed mercy on the trainer. Is this important? What does it mean to show mercy? Think of some examples of how people or animals can show mercy one to another.

Answer: Mercy is very important. When someone shows mercy, it means they have chosen to not do what they could have done. The policeman who stops a speeder, but gives them a warning instead of a ticket is showing mercy. A judge who gives a criminal probation instead of sending them to prison is showing mercy. There's even a children's game called "Mercy." There are many other examples.

4. A dog might growl or snap at an adult who grabs his tail, yet it doesn't seem to mind it much when a small child does the same thing? Why?

Answer: Dogs are pretty smart. They know that if an adult or an older child tries to hurt them, they know what they are doing. It's on purpose. But most dogs seem to sense that a baby or a really small child is not deliberately trying to hurt them. They are more tolerant. (You might want to discuss the words "tolerant" or "tolerance" with your group.)

5. Does this story contain a "second chance"? Explain. Why is it important?

> Answer: The second chance is always the "next time" that the individual has the opportunity to use the wisdom they learned from the first mistake. In this case the whale gave the trainer an opportunity for a "next time." How well the trainer used it is up to him, but the "next time" or "second chance" for this trainer and this whale will happen the next time they are in the tank together. We have a pretty hard word for folks who choose not to learn from their second chance DUMB (although in this instance there might be two words: DUMB *and* DEAD)! Second chances are very important because they give us an opportunity to learn from our mistakes.

6. Do we always have a "second chance"? If you say "No," what does it mean about how we should try to act when we are upset?

> Answer: No, we don't. If the whale had killed the trainer, there would have been no second chance. Some kids try drugs or alcohol and overdose or die behind the wheel of their car without ever having a second chance. There are folks who are killed by their first heart attack, never learning to take better care of themselves. We should always try to make the best of our *first* chance when we are upset. It is important to think about the consequences of our behavior as it could affect ourselves and others. There might not be a second chance.

7. Can you think of a time in your own life when your anger got you into serious trouble, or could have?

> Answer: Individual stories would go here.

8. Activity: "The Next Day"
Let the group take turns role-playing how the trainer might deal with the whale the next day and all the days that followed.

> Answer: This should be interesting, because it's pretty difficult to punish a killer whale. Actually, one way trainers deal with disobedient behavior is to not respond to the animal for awhile (ignoring). Sometimes they turn their back to the whale and do something else. This often results in the whale being more cooperative when the trainer comes back.

Reference:

Permission was granted for me to share the story about the killer whale provided no names were used.

To Clear the Fog

Application

This story is intended to help youngsters discern between perception and reality, especially when they are *not* the same.

Prologue

Canasta

When I was a small child, I had an experience that was real to me, although a big part of it wasn't real at all.

My folks enjoyed playing card games back then, their favorite being Canasta. It was a community event to gather at the homes of families to play. Some evenings, we'd have as many as 3 or 4 card tables set up in the living room and kitchen. I always enjoyed these games because there were other kids to play with, and there was always plenty of great stuff to eat!

Grandma came down from Oklahoma to visit us. She slept in my bed, so I bunked on the couch in the living room.

I awoke in the middle of the night. At first, I was confused, being on the couch and not in my bed. Confusion turned to fear when I saw that the card players, including my mother and father, were still there, playing away! They had not been there when Mom made my bed on the couch. I tried to speak to them, but they did not respond. They just kept on laughing and talking and playing Canasta.

Confusion and fear became panic; I cried out for my father. He came running down the hall and flipped on the light.

There were no card tables; there were no card players, just me in my bed on the couch (except by this time the sheets and blankets were on the floor). Dad reassured me; I had experienced a nightmare. Things were really okay and as they should be.

I wasn't convinced. When he turned out the light and headed back to bed, I pulled the covers up over my head so I wouldn't have to see the Canasta players. And I slept with the covers over my head (even in the summer, with no air-conditioning) for many years after that.

Why Not?

Why wouldn't youngsters have a little trouble sorting out what they perceive and believe from what they *know* to be real? When a person is 5 years old, we encourage their beliefs in Santa Claus and the Easter Bunny, yet consider the same individual to be out-of-touch if they subscribe to the same beliefs 10 years later.

As the following story will illustrate, perception and reality are usually closely connected—but not always. Perception can never be a fitting substitute for reality, regardless of how much we might want it to be. We can use desire and initiative to act in such a way as to alter reality, but we cannot change it simply by denying it exists.

But it is precisely at this level of perception where distressed youngsters can be helped the most. For instance, children who are afraid of the dark are comforted little by adults who tell them, "There's nothing to be afraid of in the dark!" Pretty silly; if such youngsters really believed that to be true, they wouldn't be afraid in the first place. In this instance, reality is fine. Perception is the problem. Here our focus should be the fear, not the darkness.

I have heard many teens tell me that their parents and teachers did not care about them, even though I was convinced that it was simply not the case at all. Here's another situation where healing would come best not from arguing reality ("Of course I love you," a frustrated parent screams at their child; a fruitless venture that will create more heat than light), but in helping bring about the small changes that the youngster is capable of perceiving, such as non-verbal gestures of affirmation, or a surprise small gift. When you get really good at this, they call you a therapist.

Whenever perception and reality are in conflict, work on perception first. It's the best way to clear the fog.

The Story (To Clear the Fog)

It's getting darker ... and colder. I try to coax a little more speed out of the rental car, closing the distance between Gillette and the Black Hills.

17

I guess I had always known that Mount Rushmore was in South Dakota. It didn't occur to me that I was so close to the place until I landed in Rapid City and saw on display in the terminal the whole story of Gutzon Borglum and his amazing feat of artistry and engineering.

I decided that, if I could make it back in time after my program in Gillette, I'd visit Mount Rushmore National Memorial.

Turning south off I-90, I head for Keystone. With elevation the light snow turns to fine crystals of ice. It's completely dark now, but I was told that the great stone sculptures of Washington, Jefferson, Roosevelt and Lincoln are lit at night, making the view perhaps even more spectacular.

The road steepens as it leaves Keystone. Ice is collecting on bridges as I press on. I arrive at the entrance to the park site and pull into the underground part of the huge parking lot. I grab my camera from my carry-on bag and chug up several sets of stairs to the Avenue of Flags and walk out onto the Grandview Terrace. I take a look.

Fog! I strain to see the men in the mountain. Nothing. All I see is a thick blanket of grayness; not even the powerful floodlights can punch through it.

All I had seen and read told me that squarely in front of me is one of the most stunning collaborations of man and nature. But I can't see it. The mountain *is* there; I just can't see it.

It *Is* What It *Is*

I returned to Rapid City that night and to my home the next morning. In reflecting on my disappointment, I realized a truth about reality: It is what it is—whether we see it, believe it, or accept it or not.

I considered how arrogant it would have been for me to believe that, since I could not see the presidents that night, they did not exist. Such thinking would have been wrong. Seven months later, I was there again. That time I saw them.

Mount Rushmore National Memorial

The Black Hills of South Dakota form the backdrop for Mount Rushmore. The 60-foot-high faces of presidents Washington, Jefferson, Roosevelt and Lincoln are 500 feet up. Sculptor Gutzon Borglum began drilling into the 6,200-foot high mountain in 1927. Officially called the "Shrine to Democracy," the project took 14 years to complete at a cost of $1 million.

Today it's considered priceless.

Questions/Activities

1. Have you ever heard of Mount Rushmore? Have you ever seen a picture of it? Describe it. Have you ever been there?

Answer: Responses will vary.

2. Let's say you knew a person who said that they went to see Mount Rushmore and all they saw was fog. What would you think if they told you they didn't think it was there simply because they couldn't see it?

Answer: Pretty close-minded. Such a person would have difficulty with lots of things if they believe they must see or experience something for it to be true.

3. Does that mean that we know some things are true even when we cannot experience them personally?

Answer: Who wants to be bitten by a rattlesnake to learn it can really hurt you? Is it necessary to drown in order to learn that you can't breathe underwater? We can't really see air, but planes fly in it. There have been lots of things happen in history that we believe, although we were not there to experience them personally. We learn about lots of things that we might never experience.

4. Is it difficult sometimes to admit that something is real when we don't want it to be? Can you think of any examples?

Answer: It can be very difficult. When a person is told that a loved one has died, they often don't believe it right away. Most any kind of bad news is difficult to take at first.

5. What would you say about a person whose grandmother has died, and they say that she isn't really dead?

Answer: They are having trouble accepting the news.

6. Which would be more of a problem: a person believing for 3 days that their grandmother did not die, or a person believing it for 3 years?

Answer: It's not unusual for denial to simply fade away in a short period of time. Sometimes short-term denial gives a child or adolescent a bit of time to process the full impact of the news. A person who is in denial for 3 years is in trouble. Denial of reality is not always a serious problem if the person is doing all right at home, school and relationships.

7. Would it help to scream at this person, telling them that they are wrong? What should you do?

Answer: Screaming like this might only serve to make things worse, perhaps causing the person to become even more upset or afraid. We should continue to be friends with them and try to help them.

8. It was mentioned that we sometimes cannot see or experience something for ourselves. We must depend on others to tell us what is real, or what really happened. Do you know someone who, if they told you that something happened, you would believe them completely? Why would you believe that person?

Answer: Yes, people like parents, grandparents, uncles or aunts, friends and teachers. One reason why we believe them is because we trust them. We know they care enough about us not to lie to us.

9. Activity: Line Puzzle

Draw this line puzzle on the board or on a large piece of paper. Ask the group, "Which line is longer?"

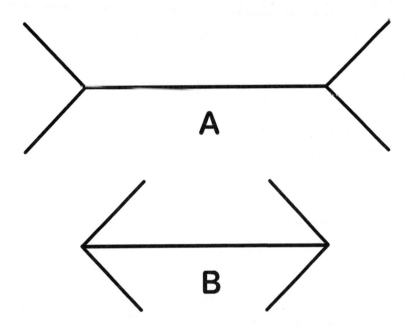

Answer: They are identical in length.

10. Why does line "A" look longer than line "B"?

Answer: It looks longer because of how the environment at the ends of the line is structured.

11. In life, can our "environment" cause us to be perceived differently?

Answer: Of course. If a person hangs out with losers and troublemakers, they are going to be branded the same.

12. Activity: Square Puzzle

Draw this square puzzle on the board or a large piece of paper. Ask, "How many squares are there?"

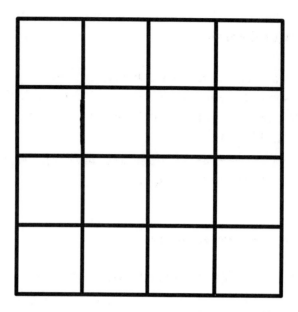

Answer: Actually, there are 30. There are 16 on the inside, and 1 big one on the outside, making 17. Combining squares into 4s, there are 3 across and 3 down, making 9 more, for a total of 26. Then, when you group them into squares containing 9 smaller squares (3x3 each), 4 will fit, making a total of 30.

13. What is the message hidden in this puzzle?

Answer: Sometimes there's more to something than what we see at first.

14. Activity: Find the "F"s

Put this sentence on a piece of paper and give one to each person in the group. Ask them to count the "F"s in the passage.

FINISHED FILES ARE THE RESULT OF YEARS OF SCIENTIFIC STUDY COMBINED WITH THE EXPERIENCE OF YEARS.

Answer: There are actually six (finished, files, of, of, scientific, of). Most folks look right past the "F"s in the "of"s because they are actually pronounced with a "v" sound, as in "uv."

15. What is the message hidden in this puzzle?

> Answer: It's pretty much the same message as the square puzzle. At first glance, we tend to miss details that are right in front of us.

16. Activity: "Through the Hole"

Take a sheet of paper and fold it so that you can tear a quarter-sized hole in the center. Hold up the paper and announce that you will now push Jimmy or Mary (or any other member of the class or group) through the hole in the piece of paper. Of course they'll laugh, saying it cannot be done.

Then, simply put your finger through the hole and push the person. You have just done *exactly* what you said you were going to do.

17. What is the message hidden in this puzzle?

> Answer: This puzzle plays on thought instead of vision, but it demonstrates well the idea that there's more than one way to accomplish something. Encourage your youngsters to look for them.

18. Activity: "Number or Letter?"

Make up two signs like the ones shown here, one of numbers, and one of letters. Note that the center figure in both groups is the same. Then, make another sign of just the center figure. That's a total of three signs.

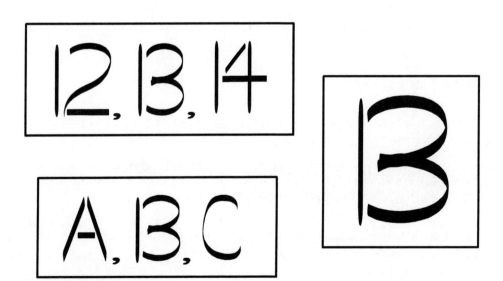

Break the class or group into two, group A and group B. Have group A hide their eyes as you show group B only the sign of numbers. Then have group B hide their eyes as you show group A only the sign of letters. Put both of the signs away, and have both groups give you their attention. Tell them that you are going to show them something, and you want them to all quickly shout out what they see.

Show them the sign with the single figure. Half the group will shout out "13!" and half will shout out "B!" Show them how you set up their different responses.

19. What is the message hidden in this puzzle?

Answer: Environment and context, plus how we are set up to believe, makes a great difference in how and what we perceive. In this example each group was "conditioned" to see the last sign differently. Discuss what this might mean in everyday life.

20. Activity: Dead or Alive?

Sometimes perception can be changed by the way we emphasize a word. For instance, show the group this statement, and tell them that the patient can be dead or alive by the way we say the following sentence:

"DOCTOR, THAT PATIENT WOULD HAVE DIED IF YOU HADN'T OPERATED ON HIM!"

21. Ask the group to get into teams and repeat this statement that makes the patient still alive.

Answer: "DOCTOR, THAT PATIENT WOULD HAVE *DIED* IF YOU HADN'T OPERATED ON HIM!"

22. Ask them to do it again, this time noting that the patient is dead.

Answer: "DOCTOR, THAT PATIENT WOULD HAVE DIED IF YOU *HADN'T* OPERATED ON HIM!"

23. What is the hidden message in this word game?

Answer: Be careful what you say, and how you say it.

References:

Most of the puzzles and brain-teasers are readily available through a number of sources. I learned the "Find the 'F's" activity from the late Dr. Bob Lindbergh of San Antonio, Texas, a much-respected psychologist and fellow speaker. The "Dead or Alive?" activity was a favorite teaching tool of Dr. Empress Zedler. For many years, she was Director of the Department of Special Education at Southwest Texas State University in San Marcos, Texas. She used the activity to stress the importance of oral language structure in conveying content and meaning.

Just Ask!

Application

This story helps us understand that, in order to deal with some challenges in life, we need to ask for some help.

Prologue

Ever wonder why many folks never ask for help with a problem? It seems that we never seek help in pulling up the weeds of life until *after* they've gone to seed.

For some, "HELP!" truly is a four-letter word.

It is man's nature to be helpful to others. It's a quality mingled with the others into the same genetic material that gives us eye color, baldness and an aversion to dentist's offices. In fact, Dr. Joyce Brothers once said that, to establish a relationship with another person quickly, ask them for a small favor. Folks seem to enjoy being helpful; asking benefits more than just the asker.

It does not, however, appear to be man's nature to *ask* for help. At some point individuals reach the awareness that there are things they can't do or work out themselves. That should be when we learn the value of the resources of others and the critical skill of asking for some help. (And a good thing, too. Ever consider performing your own appendectomy, or doing your own root canal?)

I believe the ability to ask comes from deep inside. It's the ability to say to self, "I'm really an okay person, and I don't have to know everything or be able to know everything or do everything to still be okay." In fact, part of being okay is having sense enough to recognize the limits. In other words, being okay means being honest with ourselves.

This story and its accompanying questions and activities help teach the value of asking.

The Story (*Just Ask!*)

I have a professional acquaintance named Lola; she lives in California. Lola is a professional speaker, a very good humorist. If you ever heard her speak, you would agree that excellence on the platform is Lola's gift.

But coordination is not. You see, Lola was born with no motor control on her left side. When walking, and especially when hurrying, she has to continually remind herself to pick up her feet. Her greatest obstacle is one of rushing to make connecting flights in airports. In fact, she used refer to her busiest speaking season as the "fall season," because that's what Lola did a lot of—falling.

One day, perhaps it was after an especially painful and embarrassing airport tumble, Lola glanced down the concourse and saw the little shuttle cart whisking passengers from one flight to another. She stopped the driver.

"What do I have to do to be able to ride in your cart to my gate?" she asked.

"Nothing," came the reply. "All you have to do is ask. Would you like a ride?"

It was that simple. Lola shares, "lately, I've been asking. And I've been getting."

For Lola the "fall season" has just about completely disappeared.

Good things come to those who ask.

Attitude: The Other Part

Martha Berry was a prominent educator from the mountains of northwestern Georgia. She set about to establish a school for poor students who wanted to continue their education after public school (which, at the time, was pretty limited). It didn't mean that things were going to be easy; they had to work hard at the school. But they didn't have to worry about coming up with the hard cash to attend.

The school was successful alright, but Mrs. Berry had a difficult time keeping it going. She needed some help. As it worked out, she was to attend a big function, a fancy dinner. Henry Ford, one of the richest men in America at the time, was on the guest list. She reasoned that Mr. Ford knew what it was like to be poor; she wanted him to know about her special school. She decided that she would ask him for a donation. She planned to ask Mr. Ford for $1 million!

And that's exactly what she did. Mr. Ford hesitated for a moment, then reached into his pocket and handed Mrs. Berry a dime. A dime!

Martha Berry didn't flinch. She graciously accepted Mr. Ford's 10 cents and thanked him for it. She tied it up in the corner of her handkerchief and slipped it into her purse.

Back at her school, Mrs. Berry called two of the mountain boys into her office. She gave them the dime. "I want you to go down to the feed and seed store and buy exactly 10 cents worth of peanut seed with this dime," she instructed. "Not 9 cents, and not 11 cents, but *exactly* 10 cents."

They did; she instructed them to plant the peanuts. That crop was used for seed again. The second crop was packaged into small bags and sold at a crossroads store for 10 cents a bag. They took in $300, with which Mrs. Berry purchased a piano for the music department of the school.

Mrs. Berry wrote a letter to Mr. Ford, explaining what she had done with his dime. By return mail, she received a train ticket to Detroit and an invitation to be the house guest of Henry and Clara Ford. During her visit, Mr. Ford presented Martha Berry a check for $1 million.

Berry College stands today as testimonial to this woman and her remarkable vision.

Questions/Activities

1. In the first story, Lola fell down a lot in airports. Why did it take her so long to ask to ride the cart?

Answer: Who knows for sure without asking her, but maybe she was embarrassed to ask. Maybe she was afraid to ask. Maybe she felt silly asking.

2. Do people sometimes have trouble asking for a favor or for some help?

Answer: They certainly do!

3. Is it good to ask for help sometimes? Are there some things we cannot do for ourselves?

Answer: Yes it is; it creates humility and deepens relationships. There are often things we cannot do for ourselves. Asking is the key to getting them done.

4. Can we learn to be more comfortable asking for a favor or for help?

Answer: Yes, but it takes practice.

5. Is it possible to ask too much?

Answer: Yes it is, for several reasons.
A. If we ask too much, it might mean that we are not trying to do more ourselves.
B. It could make a person too dependent on the help of others.
C. People who ask, ask, ask all the time soon develop the reputation of being a pest.

6. Did Mrs. Berry have the right to be upset with Mr. Ford when he gave her only a dime?

>Answer: Probably; many people would have been upset with him, whether they said or did anything about it or not.

7. What would have happened if Mrs. Berry had been upset with Mr. Ford?

>Answer: She would have made a $1 million mistake, wouldn't she? That would have affected many more people than Mrs. Berry.

8. What can we learn from this story about Mrs. Berry?

>Answer: How we handle disappointment can make a big difference in long-term outcomes.

9. Activity: Role Play

Break the class or group into smaller groups. Let one group role play the scene like it might have been with Lola and the cart driver in the airport. Then let the groups brainstorm other scenes and ways to ask for what you need (such as getting directions, asking for medical assistance, or asking for a hand with a door when your arms are full). Role play these.

10. Activity: "How 'bout it, Mr. Ford?"

Role play the Martha Berry story. Then, role play other ways it could have happened if Mrs. Berry had handled it differently.

11. Activity: "How it used to be"

In discussing the benefits and strengths of asking others for a favor, for information, or for assistance with something, consider what a funeral was like just a couple or three generations ago. Back then it was the responsibility of the family of the deceased to prepare the body for burial, to make the coffin themselves, to conduct the wake and funeral, and to bury the dearly departed. Would anyone want to try that today?

12. Activity: "Ask-tivities"

Write the names of each member of the class or group on small slips of paper, and have each person draw a slip. During the next one to three days, they are to ask a favor of some sort from the person whose name they drew. They are to write down when and where they asked the favor, who they asked, what they asked for, and what happened next (here's a form to help). Finally, set aside some time for some sharing. For instance, let them answer this question: "Was it easier to do the asking, or to help someone who asked? Why?"

Ask-tivity Form

Name:

Date:

_____

Whom did you ask?

Where did you ask (place, day and time)?

What did you ask for?

What happened?

What did you learn?

References:

Lola is Lola Gillebaard of Laguna Beach, California. I was so touched by her article, "The Fall Gal" (*Professional Speaker* magazine, October, 1992), I used it, with Lola's permission, in the Fall, 1993, issue of my newsletter, *Reaching Out.* It is used here again with her permission.

The Martha Berry story was told in a sermon by Rev. Charles L. Woodward, pastor of Trinity Baptist Church in Pleasanton, Texas. A descendant of Martha Berry later came up to me at a program and verified the story. It has several "spins," but it is true.

The Rose

Application

This story is for use with the child or adolescent who is experiencing an intense sense of loss of a close loved one. It also doubles to help a group of youngsters understand the nature of death and how best to deal with it.

Prologue

Life is fragile; loss is a tough thing to handle. Experiences of loss lead to sadness (depression) just like standing in the rain leads to getting wet. In fact, experts generally agree that all reactive depression is about a loss of some sort ("reactive" simply means that the depression is tied to a specific situation or circumstance, as compared, for instance, to depression caused by chemical imbalance).

I agree, also (although words like "all" bother me a bit). Many things can be lost. There are the obvious losses, such as the loss of a home, a job or a loved one, but there are less tangible losses, such as the loss of security, confidence, relationships, lifestyle and personal identity. The fact that they are less tangible losses makes them no less traumatic to experience. And consider this: it is possible to be very depressed and not know why (sometimes referred to as "repression").

This story was written for the support and recovery from a very difficult loss, the loss of a loved one. The patient was 11 years old when I began working with her. Her father was terminally ill with cancer. The strain of the situation worsened as her mother took the father off on extended trips for treatment in different parts of the country. The blow of the father's death was eased considerably by the family's willingness and desire to prepare this, their youngest child, for his loss. He was marvelous. He talked to her honestly, and even wrote letters for her to keep. Naturally, however, his passing was still deeply painful for her.

I wrote this story for her, comparing the life of her father to a flower.

The Story (*The Rose*)

Once I put a rose in a bud vase. It was new and fresh, just beginning to unfold. In several days it was in full bloom. It was fragrant; it was beautiful. It was real.

In a few days, I noticed that, slowly, one at a time, the petals began to fall from the rose.

It was not beautiful anymore. It was dying.

I didn't want it to die. I wanted to keep its beauty for myself forever. But it died anyway.

"I know," I exclaimed. "I know how to have a rose and have it stay in bloom. I will buy for myself an artificial one." And that's what I did.

It was a beautiful flower, but it had no fragrance. It was perfectly formed, but it had no texture when I touched it. It plastic; it could never be real.

Daddy, you were so much like a rose. When I was little, you were my always and forever hero. You were bigger than life; you were strong and kind. You were smart, sensitive, loving, warm and real.

But then you became ill; your strength began to fail. The pain in your eyes told me you were fighting for your life. I had to stand helplessly by as a petal fell. Fear clutched me as I realized that you really might die.

Then, the day came when the very last petal fell. You slipped away, and I knew that I would never again see you in this world. The pain was almost too much to stand.

It was then I realized something. I realized that, even with all its petals gone, the remains of the most beautiful flower contain something very special. Deep inside lie the seeds. Inside are the beginnings of life that follow and carry on.

Daddy, I am *your* seed. I am a strong seed, and I am full of life because of you and Mom.

A plastic flower would never produce any seed. You were real. I love you so much.

Questions/Activities

1. Does experience matter? Would a 16-year-old have less trouble dealing with the loss of a loved one than a 6-year-old?

Answer: This is generally true. As children grow older, they become more adaptive, understanding that these things happen. They also know how they dealt with an earlier experience. Very young children have had few experiences of deep loss, so they often are "lost" for awhile in dealing with it. They rely on the experience and reassurance of loved ones to help them move through the loss.

2. Did this 11-year-old girl really understand that her father was dying?

Answer: Maybe not so much at first, but in her case she had a little time to take it all in. Sometimes, when a loved one dies instantly (as in a car wreck), the loss is more difficult to absorb.

3. Did the girl's father do the right thing in trying to prepare her for his death?

Answer: Absolutely.

4. Have you ever been to a funeral? What happens at a funeral? If a friend needed to attend a funeral, but had never been to one, how would you tell them to act?

Answer: Explain the process of a funeral. Reassure the friend that funerals are a passage of life, like birth and marriage. Just act in a quiet, respectful way, and pay attention to the adults who are with you. They will show you what you need to know.

5. What do you say to a friend who has just lost a loved one?

Answer: What you say is not nearly as important as saying *something*. Too often, people feel that, if they said anything, it would only make the person more sad. This is not true. They are sad already, so your support lets them know you care. If you say nothing, and they know you know, they might feel that you don't care. The best thing to say is something simple and heartfelt, like: "Mary, I was sorry to hear that your grandmother died. Please let me know if I can help you in any way."

6. Activity: Delicate and Perishable

This story suggests that flowers are a thoughtful gift because they are lovely and valued. The fact that they are delicate or perishable establishes their value (it might be helpful to discuss "perishable"). How many other things can you think of which make excellent gifts because they are delicate or perishable? Tell also what makes them special:

Answer: Here are a few suggestions. You might want to set up a display of these things:
Fine Crystal: It is very delicate and breakable.
Porcelain and China: These are also delicate and breakable.
Polished Silver: It is a precious metal, but it will tarnish.
A Basket of Peaches: They are delicious, but peaches will spoil if not eaten soon.
A Pitcher of Cream: Rich and tasty, but cream will sour and become rancid.
Fine Linen: It is lovely, but it can tear and can become soiled.
An Antique Painting: It is beautiful, but delicate. It must be handled carefully.

7. I once worked with a teacher who shared delicate and perishable things all the time with her class. She taught at a school in a very poor community. At Christmas, she put very expensive glass ornaments (that she found in Germany) on her classroom Christmas tree. She was an artist and decorated her classroom with oil paintings, and her husband brought his prized orchids to school and showed them to her class. None of these things were ever damaged or destroyed in her classroom. Why?

Answer: These youngsters enjoyed the opportunity to experience the things. And, with her guidance, they learned to respect them not only for their beauty, but for their delicate and perishable nature. Everyone benefited.

8. Activity: Pet Memorial

For a young person, the first loss of a living thing is usually the loss of a pet. When my son was in high school, he kept a picture of a favorite cat taped to his bathroom mirror. He and that old cat had enjoyed a special relationship.

Here is an interesting activity. Conduct a favorite pet memorial service. Encourage each student to bring a picture of the pet they lost, or encourage them to draw a picture of them and the pet playing together. Since the idea here is the loss of the pet, not necessarily the death of the animal, pets that ran away, had to be given away or just disappeared would also represent a loss.

9. Activity: "I Remember _____ Day"

The loss of a grandparent or a great-grandparent is usually the first loss of a family member for school-aged youngsters. In fact, such a loss, or the fear of an impending loss, can bring on significant behavioral change in the youngster (fortunately, it's usually temporary). When my mother was very ill with cancer and in the hospital, my 9-year-old daughter became belligerent and difficult in her attitudes and behaviors. This was not like her at all. Although she recovered quickly, things were difficult at the time. (This is an example of why we need to look at the reasons for inappropriate behavior, instead of blatantly punishing the symptoms. I remember a television program about a young teen who brought a gun to school and gave it to a teacher because he was afraid that, if he left it at home, his despondant mother would have shot herself with it. Although it is wrong to bring guns to school, the boy was attempting to preserve life through his action, not take life. Perhaps he could have handled the situation another way, but, if his story checked out, his intent was clear. Intent makes all the difference; ask any attorney.)

As an activity, have an "I Remember _____Day," with the child's name for that person going in the blank. Make a big production of this, with a banner and everything. Send out invitations to parents, relatives and other adults to attend. Set up a table at the front of the classroom or meeting room, and cover it with a tablecloth. Place candles and a flower vase on the table. Have some inexpensive flowers available (a flower shop might even donate some), or allow the youngsters to bring their own.

Again, like with the pets, encourage the youngsters to bring pictures of their "I Remember" person, and let them share their favorite story about that person. Since some youngsters will never have lost a grandparent or a family member that they knew well, it would be appropriate for them to talk about a deceased relative they would liked to have known (a great way for a youngster to brush up on family history).

At the conclusion of the presentation, each youngster places a flower in the vase. After the service, the vase of flowers can be delivered to a local hospital or to a rest home.

Here is a sample story about my grandmother and me.

Grandma and the train ride

For a number of years, I was the only grandchild on my mother's side of the family. My grandmother and I were close. (Hey, when you're the *only* one, you get lots of attention.)

One of my favorite memories of Grandma goes back to when she and I spent most of the summer with my aunt's family in Minnesota. I was about nine at the time. At the end of the summer, Grandma and I made the return trip to Tulsa, Oklahoma, by train. Those were the days when only the well-to-do could even think of traveling by air.

We were well prepared. Stocked with a couple of sacks of books, games and plenty of snacks, Grandma and I boarded the train and settled in for the two-day trip. I can still remember watching the scenery go by, and drifting in and out of sleep to the rhythm of the clickity-clack of steel wheels on steel rails.

For those folks riding through the night in coach (instead of the more expensive Pullman cars), the porter would make his way down the aisle renting pillows. We only needed one. Grandma, an experienced rail traveler, always brought along a huge, down pillow.

In the morning, the train made a stop (in St. Louis, as I recall), so Grandma treated me to a hearty breakfast in the station cafe. When we reboarded and returned to our coach seats, we discovered that the porter had taken up *all* the pillows! She insisted that the porter sort through the piles and piles of pillows until he found the one that belonged to her. He finally brought her *a* pillow, but it wasn't *the* pillow (something he heard about all the way to Tulsa).

Thinking back, I suppose traveling by train with my grandmother stands out in my mind because it was a special adventure the two of us shared. Through the years, we did a lot of things together. Grandma even taught me how to embroider a little and bake sugar cookies. (We decided once to triple the recipe, and had more cookies than we could find jars, cans and boxes to put them in; but that's *another* story.)

I was home on leave from the US Navy when my grandmother passed away in 1968. It was a few days before my scheduled departure for a 2-year hitch in Japan. She was very sick, but she knew I was still home. To this day, I believe she picked her time; she waited for me to come home.

I've heard of these things happening.

10. Activity: What If?

As an activity, encourage your group to think of what the world would be like if nothing, humans or critters, ever died.

> Answer: Here are a few thought-jolters. Of course, this represents just a starting point. It could be expanded considerably.
> A. First of all, the earth and air would be thick with every gnat, fly, mosquito and insect imaginable.
> B. There would be a tremendous overabundance of domestic and wild animals. There wouldn't be enough food to feed them, so many would be starving. City streets would be full of dogs and cats, and animal control would be a serious problem.
> C. Overpopulation of people would create shortages of housing.
> D. Unemployment would be staggering.
> E. Adequate health care would be a problem due to the sheer number of people.
> F. Hospitals and rest homes would be bursting at the seams trying to house an ever-growing population of elderly. Financially, we would be hard-pressed to pay for this care.
> G. Because of the need to build more stores, restaurants, health care facilities and housing, we would have less room to grow crops to feed humans and livestock. This, as well as population problems, would likely create significant food shortages.
> H. There would probably be no way to feed everyone adequately.

11. From the discussion generated in response to question #4, ask your students to break up into smaller groups, with a direction for each subgroup to come up with a conclusion about the notion of death.

Answer: Death is a natural and necessary part of the balance of nature.

References:

The person that shared paintings, orchids, delicate ornaments and many other treasures with her students was Rebecca Adler, a master teacher and a marvelous human being. Her influence extended far beyond the lesson for the day.

The story about the train ride with my grandmother is from *GRAND-Stories* by Ernie Wendell (Pleasanton, TX: Friendly Oaks Publications, 2000). The story and the illustration are included here with permission.

The story, "The Rose," is from the original *Windows* by James Sutton (Pleasanton, TX: Friendly Oaks Publications, 1991).

An Answer For The King

Application

This story, with its questions and activities are intended to help youngsters understand the nature, scope and outcomes of genuine character.

Prologue

I was having lunch with a most respected friend when the topic of character entered our conversation. He observed that, at the onset, our young country produced towering figures in character and leadership; figures like Washington, and, a bit later, Lincoln. My friend then noted that, although the population of our country has increased exponentially since the day of these great leaders, it seems that we are hard-pressed to produce individuals of like character. What is the problem? (By the way, the friend is Zig Ziglar. I believe he is right on target in his observation).

Do we live in an age of character convenience, where we can change our convictions as we would change a pair of shoes? Is it difficult to teach youngsters about character when it seems rare to observe it in daily practice? Is character relegated to a seat somewhere behind MTV and the World Wrestling Federation?

What we're really talking about is a commitment that comes from the marrow of the bone. It's a "This is right; this is wrong; I know the difference" commitment that takes a stand—whatever it takes.

Here's a story I adapted from an account in Napoleon Hill's classic book, *Think and Grow Rich*. It should generate some interesting discussion.

The Story (*An Answer for the King*)

When the young Colonies (early America) were looking to the Crown (King George of England) for the rights and freedoms afforded British subjects in England, one figure stood above all the rest—Samuel Adams.

Adams and his freedom-minded constituents were such an irritant to King George that a representative was dispatched to the Colonies, a Governor Gage. Gage's job was to stamp out all insurrection before it grew even stronger.

But Governor Gage was no fool. He knew that Adams had the ear, the heart, and the support of many in the Colonies. "Better to recruit him than to fight him," Gage must have thought as he pondered how to deal with Adams. So he sent a military officer, a Colonel Fenton, to pay a visit to Adams.

"Sir, I have been sent by Governor Gage to reason with you. Mr. Adams, I am authorized to inform you that, should you make your peace with the King, you will be generously rewarded," Fenton said. "But if you insist in leading these activities of insurrection, we will, in time, seize you, try you for treason against the Crown, and publicly hang you by your neck until you are dead. Mr. Adams, when you have an answer for the Governor, send for me, and I will convey it for you."

With that, Colonel Fenton turned to leave.

"Colonel," Adams said calmly, "there is no need to wait. You may have my answer right now. You may tell Governor Gage that I, Samuel Adams, have long since made my peace with the King of Kings, and that no amount of personal consideration shall dissuade me from this right and righteous cause."

And that's the message Colonel Fenton took back to Governor Gage.

Adams had signed his statement with his life. Had America failed to achieve victory in the Revolutionary War, Sam Adams would have been executed.

———————————————

Questions/Activities

1. What's the big deal anyway? Don't we have freedom of speech in this country?

Answer: We do now, but not back then. Colonel Fenton probably could have shot Adams to death right there on the porch of his own home. Sam Adams had put everything he had into his answer—including his life.

2. But wasn't Mr. Adams a little scared?

Answer: Perhaps. But if he was, he didn't let fear change him or his answer.

3. What is freedom of speech anyway?

Answer: The Constitution guarantees you the right to have an opinion on just about anything. And it gives you the right to express your opinion without fear of consequence from the government. But this freedom is not absolute. You can't say anything you like, especially if you threaten the safety or the lives of others. For instance, a person could say, "I think it's unfair to have to pay income tax to the government," and even wear a signboard on the street corner as they say it. But they can't yell "Fire!" in a crowded movie theater when there isn't one.

4. Activity: What is the Difference (Part I)?

Put the youngsters into groups, and let them come up with some answers to this question: **What is the difference between strong character and just plain stubbornness?**

Answer:
A. The depth of principles and values involved
B. The endurance of the principles and values (lasting or short-term)
C. Benefits to others, not just self
D. The creation of a better person

5. Activity: What is the Difference (Part II)?

Let the groups work on this question: **What is the difference between courage and character?**

Answer: Although it takes courage to exercise true character, it is possible to exercise courage without character (depending, perhaps, on a rather liberal definition of courage). It might take some courage for a person to steal a car or rob a bank, but such behavior does not reflect character.

6. Activity: How can we exercise character?

Answer:
A. By determining how we will handle frustration and disappointment.
B. By enduring short-term pain for long-term principle.
C. By not going with the crowd when the crowd is wrong.

7. Activity: *A Man for All Seasons* (for older groups)

Show and discuss the movie, *A Man for All Seasons* (Best Picture, 1966), or share the story of Sir Thomas More. There are strong similarities between More and Sam Adams.

In this true story, More is chancellor of England. A devout Catholic, More refuses to support King Henry VIII's divorce (so that he can marry his mistress). The king splits with Rome and the Pope, and More resigns his office in protest. The king then establishes himself as the head of the Church of England. When Sir Thomas More refuses to acknowledge the king as the head of the church, he is thrown into prison. Eventually More elects to be beheaded rather than publicly sanction the king's actions.

Reference:

Hill, N., *Think and Grow Rich*. New York: Fawcett Crest, 1960.

The Power of Belief

Application

This story helps us realize the power of belief.

Prologue

There's a standing joke in the mental health profession about the psychiatric patient who was convinced that he was dead. He would talk and argue for hours about how he had been dead for years. No one could convince him otherwise.

A new resident figured to crack this foolishness; he sat down with the patient.

"I understand you're dead?"

"That's right," the patient shared, beaming. "Been dead ever since I can remember."

"Tell me, then," said the resident, "do dead people bleed?"

"Of course not! Dead people don't bleed."

With that the young doctor pricked the patient's finger. A small droplet of blood appeared.

"Son of a gun!" exclaimed the patient. "I guess dead people *do* bleed!"

It's a silly story, but it makes a point. Beliefs and realities are one and the same for some folks. To try to change their beliefs is to seriously mess with their lives.

Children, because they lack the depth of experience of adults, are even more vulnerable to the power of belief. If they believe something is true, then it's true. I know; when I was in the 3rd grade, I was convinced that I was going to die. Since that's been 48 years ago, I suppose the belief wasn't that real after all, but it did seem so at the time.

As boys will do, I got into a duel, a sword fight with sharpened pencils. A piece of lead broke off in the palm of my right hand. It bled a little, and hurt like the dickens. One of my friends casually noted that, since I now had lead in my body, it was only a matter of time before I would get lead poisoning and die. It was Wednesday; he figured me to be dead by Saturday. (By the way, the stuff in the middle of a pencil isn't really lead at all; it's graphite. But it is difficult to sort that out when you think you're dying.)

I didn't tell my teacher and I didn't go to the nurse. I was afraid they would only confirm my impending death. (Note: kids often don't want to talk about strong negative beliefs, especially life-threatening ones, for this very reason. This is one of the few times in counseling where I lead with questions that encourage "yes" or "no" answers as a more comfortable way of getting to the core of the pain.)

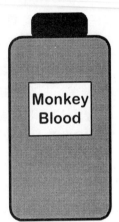

Monkey Blood

I fell apart when I got home. I told my father. He reassured me that I was going to make it. He even underscored his confidence in my recovery by administering the "cure" to the palm of my hand—something he called Monkey Blood. It burned like the dickens, his assurance that it was chasing out all the "lead bugs." I was going to live after all!

I carry a permanent graphite "tattoo" in the palm of my right hand. It's remains for me a subtle reminder of the awesome power of belief.

Three Stories (*The Power of Belief*)

Mark Twain (whose real name was Samuel Clemens) wrote a wonderful series of books about life along the Mississippi in earlier years. He was also a wonderful speaker, and much in demand around the country for his skill at storytelling.

Mr. Twain accepted an invitation from a family one summer evening to be their house guest. It was a very warm evening as he went to bed. He woke up in the middle of the night and could not go back to sleep. There was no breeze at all. Frustrated, he threw a shoe through the window. He heard the glass shatter and felt a cool breeze fill the room. Soon he was fast asleep.

When he woke the next morning, Mr. Twain discovered that he had not hit the window with the shoe at all. It was still shut! He had thrown the shoe through a glass bookcase. The only breeze he felt during the night was the breeze he had expected.

A No-brainer

Sometimes our beliefs affect how we feel about ourselves. I remember doing some testing with a young man who was having a lot of trouble in school. He was failing.

This boy had undergone surgery for the removal of a brain tumor. The surgery was successful and he was expected to fully recover with no other difficulties or problems. Yet, he was having a lot of trouble in school.

I asked him what he knew about the surgery. He told me that it was his understanding that the surgeon removed his brain—the whole thing! No wonder he was having trouble; he thought he was having to try to learn with no brain at all!

When I explained to him that he still had his brain (all of it, but without the tumor), he was surprised and delighted. His grades began improving immediately and he was happier. Almost overnight he became a better student, son and friend.

The Eyes Have It

Our beliefs can affect how we treat others. Years ago, a teacher in the midwest ran an experiment on her class. She told her class that all the students with blue eyes were smarter than the students with brown eyes. Not only did the blue-eyed students start doing better in their work than the brown-eyed ones, they became downright mean in the way they acted toward the brown-eyed students.

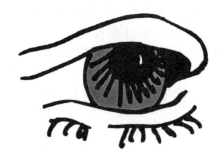

At this point the teacher did something very interesting. She told her students that she had been wrong, that actually the brown-eyed students were the smarter group. In a few days everything shifted. The brown-eyed students began doing better work, and they started putting down the blue-eyed students. It became such a problem in the classroom that she had to stop the experiment. That's when she told them that eye color really had nothing to do with how smart a person was. Then, the class settled down to the way it was before the experiment began.

Be careful what you believe. It can affect everything about you.

Questions/Activities

1. Why do you think Mr. Twain felt the breeze after he threw the shoe?

Answer: Because he believed he had hit the window with the shoe, and expected to feel the breeze.

2. Is belief really that strong?

Answer: Oh, yes.

3. Does something have to be true in order for us to believe it?

Answer: Of course not. Mr. Twain didn't break the window; the boy never lost his brain, and eye color had nothing to do with intelligence. Yet, they all *believed* these things were true, and based their expectations and behaviors on them as being true. There's another story about a man who accidentally got locked inside a freezer car on a railroad (the car in which they transport fresh meat). When the railroad workers found him the next day he was dead. The body showed all the symptoms of a person who had frozen to death. In truth, however, the freezer car was not operating due to an equipment failure. It was documented that the temperature inside the car never got below 44 degrees. The man froze to death because he *believed* it was supposed to happen.

4. If you thought that someone had removed your brain, do you think it would change your behavior?

Answer: Absolutely.

5. Perception was discussed earlier in this book. What is the difference between perception and belief?

Answer: Perception is built upon what we experience through our senses, whereas belief represents the meaning we attach to what we perceive. In short, perception refers to how we *think*, belief to how we *know*. A child can see Santa Claus in the mall at Christmastime, but that experience is not the same as believing in Santa Claus.

6. Activity: Belief versus Faith

Assign your youngsters to their groups and have them answer this question: **"What is the difference between belief and faith?"**

Answer: Although belief and faith are very close in meaning and application, there is a difference between the two. Faith is deeper, and is usually reserved for relationships. For instance, most children not only believe, but have faith that their parents will do all they can to protect them from harm. As for belief alone, it's possible for a child to believe in the Easter Bunny without experiencing the deeper faith. (We'll look at faith in the next story.)

7. Activities: Uses for Belief

Again, let the groups brainstorm some answers to this question: **"What are some ways in which we use belief to accomplish something positive?"**

Answer: Here are four ways:
A. **Medicine**—Doctors tell us that a patient's belief that a medicine will help them is often more powerful than the medicine itself. Experiments using only sugar pill medicine (called a "placebo") have resulted in healing and wellness because the patient *believed* they would get better.
B. **Hypnosis**—Hypnosis affects one's beliefs, and has been used very effectively in things such as pain management and childbirth.
C. **Counseling**—Good counseling is about helping others collect positive beliefs that can lead to positive behaviors and positive outcomes.

D. **Entertainment**—Hollywood can make a movie about life on Mars. Although we know that the movie wasn't filmed on Mars, we are inclined to believe, for the purpose of the movie, that we are on that planet with the actors. And what about magic and illusions? We know that the magician isn't really sawing a lady in half and putting her back together again, yet we are inclined to believe it (at least temporarily) for the sake of entertainment.

References:

The story about Mr. Twain throwing the shoe and the man being locked inside a non-working freezer car came from sources I cannot identify (although I believe one or both could have been shared by the incomparable Earl Nightingale). I learned of the blue eyes, brown eyes experiment in an early college class at South Texas State University (a film). It was a powerful introduction to Expectation Theory.

5 Kernels of Corn

Application

Faith is the focus of this lesson. It is intended to help youngsters understand what faith is as it pertains to relationships, and offer them encouragement to expand their faith with gratitude.

Prologue

Faith is a vision of completeness and the ability to act on that vision alone. And it's powerful, of course.

My daughter and her husband are building a new home north of Houston. When my wife and I visited them, we went out to the homesite to check on the progress. Across the street was heavily wooded property, dense with trees and underbrush. But literally dozens of SOLD signs were planted there. No houses; no driveways; no trails. Nothing, yet someone had promised to build folks' homes there. And the folks believed they could and would do it. Faith.

Small children have more faith than anyone. I was flying into Lincoln to do some programs for the University of Nebraska. I happened to watch as a flight pulled into the jetway. A small girl was with her mother, obviously meeting her father's plane. She spied her dad coming out of the jetway; he was toting luggage in both hands. The child broke away from her mother and ran to him. As she drew close, she literally launched herself into his arms, causing him to instinctively drop his bags and catch her in mid-flight.

She knew he wouldn't let her fall. Whatever happened, she knew he would catch her. Faith.

Water the Bluebonnets

I don't know why, but it seems like the very young and the very old have the most faith. One day, my sister's 93-year-old neighbor called her over to show her something in her yard.

"They're right here," she said to my sister, Janeane. She pointed to a patch of ground.

Janeane stared at the spot. It was still dry and lifeless from winter. "What's here?" she asked.

"The bluebonnets!" (Bluebonnets are the state flower of Texas, and very pretty.) "It's been pretty dry, so I'm going to give them a little moisture. In a few weeks, you'll see them."

Then, her face took on a more serious expression. "Janeane, one of these days I won't be around to water them. Will you be sure to water these bluebonnets, please? If you do, they'll never disappoint you."

She agreed. And, sure to the wise neighbor's prediction, a few weeks later, that dry and bare piece of ground broke out in a profusion of blue and white blossoms. They were there all along. Even when things looked cold and bare, they were still there. Faith. (Although one might not have much of a relationship with flower seeds, there are plenty of folks who ascribe to a relationship with the force they believe created the seeds and the life that lies within them.)

Trust is a concept very close to faith, but I don't believe that they are same. It is possible to trust in inanimate objects, such as a ladder or a bottle of medicine, but faith is reserved for people and relationships. For instance, one can have faith in the one who built the ladder or prescribed and filled the prescription for the medication.

Grandma's Bumper Crop

Gratitude is a fit partner to faith, an act of appreciating and sharing that overflows from a thankful attitude.

As she was growing up in Kansas, my mother's mother was always the sick child in her family. Yet, with her frail health, Myrtle Harriet Smith managed to outlive all of her brothers and sisters. Perhaps it was because she always had a good heart.

It was certainly a *generous* heart.

Grandma came to spend the better part of a week with me when I was a young boy. My mother joined my father on a business trip, so it was just me and Grandma. We had fun, fellowship and lots of great food!

One day she announced that she was going to make sugar cookies.

"My favorite!" I shouted. "Please make a bunch of 'em." She did; she quadrupled the already generous receipe.

We quickly realized we had a problem. Cookies began coming out of the oven quicker than I could find plates, jars, cans and boxes to put them in. The house overflowed with her laughter as I would scurry around to find one more thing that we could stuff with cookies. The "Cookie Story" became one of her favorites, and she loved telling it.

We obviously had more cookies than *we* could eat. So Grandma grabbed her scarf and we spent the rest of the afternoon delivering fresh cookies to the neighbors.

She taught me much that week and in the weeks, months and years that followed. But one of the greatests thing my grandmother ever taught me was a life-long lesson in sharing and gratitude. And she once taught it with cookies.

The following story is powerful not only in its message, but in the fact that it is true. It would be an excellent one to share during the Thanksgiving season.

The Story (Five Kernels of Corn)

On November 11, 1620, the Mayflower dropped anchor in a natural harbor on the inside of the northern tip of Cape Cod. There it stayed. The location was not the Pilgrims' first choice; they had planned to settle near the mouth of the Hudson.

The area where the ship made landfall had belonged to the Patuxets, a fierce tribe that took intense delight in murdering anyone who would dare invade their territory. A sickness, however, had wiped them out, leaving their land free for the taking. (Other Indians, fearing "bad spirits," would have no part of it.) The Pilgrims didn't even have to clear fields for planting. They were already there for them.

Their nearest neighbors were the Wampanoags, a civilized tribe ruled by Massasoit. The chief and his people accepted the Pilgrims and helped them. Squanto, a lone survivor of the Patuxets made his home with the new inhabitants, and taught them how to survive in this new and challenging land.

Although the bounty of the summer of 1621 brought a time of heartfelt gratitude (the first Thanksgiving), the Pilgrims' obligation to repay the backers who had financed their voyage left them dangerously close to starvation. Food stores had all but disappeared.

At one point, a daily ration of food for a Pilgrim was 5 kernels of corn. With a simple faith that God would sustain them, no matter what, they pulled through. History records that not a single one of them died from starvation that winter. Not a one.

The harvest of 1623 brought a surplus of corn, so much that the Pilgrims were able to help out the Indians for a change. So joyous were they that they celebrated a second Day of Thanksgiving and again invited Massasoit to be their guest.

He came, bringing with him his wife, several other chiefs and 120 braves. All sat down to a feast of 12 venison, 6 goats, 50 hogs and pigs, numerous turkeys, vegetables, grapes, nuts, plums, puddings and pies. But, lest anyone forget, all were given their first course on an empty plate.

They were each given 5 kernels of corn.

Questions/Activities

1. Would you say that the Pilgrims were a people of faith? Are there other things that you know about them that might show their faithfulness?

Answer: We know that the Pilgrims came to this country in search of religious freedom. It took faith for them to leave their friends, property and extended families. It took faith for them to make arrangements to sail to this country. It took faith to survive the rough trip across the sea, and it certainly took faith for them to survive that first winter in America.

2. Faith means a vision of completeness, with the ability to act on the vision when everything cannot be experienced right away. There are many kinds of faith, but what do we usually think of first whenever someone mentions "faith"?

Answer: Like the Pilgrims, most first thoughts are of religions or spiritual faith. In fact, when we ask someone about their religious preference, we often say something like, "And what faith are you?"

3. All of the Pilgrims, men, women and children, were obedient to their leaders, the ones who said that each person would have to get by all winter on just 5 kernels of corn per day. Was obedience part of their faith? Was this important?

Answer: Of course it was.

4. What would have happened if even a few Pilgrims had rebelled, saying that there was no way they could stay alive on just 5 kernels of corn per day?

Answer: They would have been in serious trouble. Some, maybe even all of them, would have starved. More importantly, it would have shown that they could not work together to solve their problems.

5. Have you ever been hungry, really hungry? What's the longest you have ever gone without any food at all? What was it like?

Answer: Answers will vary, of course.

6. (Tell the story about the little girl in the Lincoln airport.) Did she know something about her daddy? Was that faith?

> Answer: She knew that her daddy loved her, and that he would protect her from harm. Of course, that's faith.

7. Most children have faith that their parents will protect them, keep them safe and defend them (even risking their own lives). Are these children right to have this kind of faith?

> Answer: All children *should* be able to have this kind of faith.

8. Do children have this same kind of faith in others? Who?

> Answers: Grandparents, aunts, uncles, teachers, the school counselor and the principal would be some examples.

9. Do children ever have reason to question their faith that a parent would protect them and defend them?

> Answer: Not often, but sometimes a parent can't or won't protect or defend their child.

10. Why?

> Answer: There can be a lot of reasons. Perhaps they have trouble with alcohol or drugs in their lives. Sometimes they have so many problems of their own that they can't help anyone else. It doesn't necessarily mean that they don't care about their children; it means that they have trouble protecting and defending them.

11. Can parents and others protect us from everything?

> Answer: They can try, but the most loving, caring adult can't be everywhere at once. It can make their job easier when we help look out for ourselves and work with our friends to make sure everyone is safe.

12. Does that mean that I can have faith in my friends, and they can have faith in me to be there for them?

>Answer: Of course, and these people, being your age, will be around for a lifetime.

13. Activity: Faith versus Trust

This activity could also be done as a question, but it might better be used to stimulate great group discussion. Assign the youngsters to their groups. Ask them to compare "faith" and "trust," and give examples.

>Answer: A lot of good input will probably surface; there are no wrong answers. The challenge encourages youngsters to consider differences in these words (otherwise, why would we have both of them in our vocabulary).
>
>As mentioned in the Prologue, it is possible to trust things that are not human. We can trust an umbrella to keep us from getting wet (well, not *too* wet), and a roadmap to direct us to our destination. But faith seems to be reserved for people and relationships. It's deeper. And, in terms of relationships, faith and trust go together beautifully. We certainly do trust those we have faith in. It is also possible that human faith and non-human trust can operate together. For instance, we trust that our repaired car will now take us where we want to go, and we had faith in the mechanic to repair it properly.
>
>Anyway, you should have some good discussion on this one.

14. Activity: The Pre-Feast

Tell the youngsters in the class or group to pretend that they are present at the big Pilgrim feast that started out with 5 kernels of corn on an empty plate. Ask them to pretend that they have been asked to make a short speech, to say a few words, as the plates with the corn are being served. Then, have them all sit at a table (together or in groups) and share what they wrote.

Reference:

The source of the story about the five kernels of corn is the book, *The Light and the Glory*, by Marshall and Manuel (Grand Rapids, MI: Fleming H. Revell, 1977).

Laiton's Bread, Scarlet's Water

Application

This story and its activities help youngsters learn the value of life, the nature of compassion, and how to demonstrate true empathy.

Prologue

Children are compassionate by nature. When my son, Jamie, was in elementary school, I took him with me on a 3-day trip to the inner-city parts of Houston. He saw people eating out of garbage cans, and it troubled him deeply. He could not understand why, in a country that could afford to send men to the moon, people had to rummage through garbage for a meal. I don't think he ever forgot what he saw and how it made him feel.

Years later, I heard about another little boy who was riding with his parents in the car. They were driving through a part of town where homeless people were sleeping on the streets. He asked his father to stop the car. He got out of the car and gave his pillow to a homeless man. That one small gesture grew. Soon, blankets, pillows, clothes and food were being provided to these folks. Eventually, a homeless shelter was started; it's still operating today.

Here's a story about compassion and conviction coming together at sea.

The Story (Laiton's Bread, Scarlet's Water)

The ship's log indicated a routine voyage to the Bahamas, a pleasant trip really. The vessel was about ready to sail, carrying a load of baked bread and other cargo from a port in

New England. Captain William Laiton looked to the last few tasks as they prepared to leave.

It was the summer of 1677. Ocean-going was dependable, and, for established trading companies, quite profitable. Laiton and his crew set sail.

They had been at sea only a few days when a problem developed. The ship began to leak, slowly at first, then so profusely that the men on the bilge pumps could not keep up. The ship was sinking; nothing could be done to prevent it from going down.

Captain Laiton and the crew transferred to the longboat, taking with them all the bread they could stuff into themselves and the boat. But their supplies of water were very short.

They drifted on the ocean for 18 days; their situation became one of life and death. Water was rationed to one teaspoonful of water per man per day. It seemed especially cruel that they would die of thirst while sitting on piles of bread.

Their boat was spotted by another ship, a vessel captained by a veteran of the seas, Samuel Scarlet. But there was a problem on his ship. Scarlet and his crew were carrying plenty of water, but they had little food. They were rationing what few stores remained.

Without a second thought, Captain Scarlet set a course to rescue Laiton and his men.

"But sir, we are half-starved ourselves," some of Scarlet's crew reminded their captain. "If we rescue them, we will surely all die of starvation, both our crew and theirs." They expressed their regret about abandoning the longboat full of men, but they saw no other way for them to survive.

Captain Scarlet continued straight for the longboat. "If we do not rescue them, they will surely die. We will take them aboard, and we will share whatever we have. Beyond that, the Almighty will provide. I will *not* leave them to die in this place."

Of course this story has a joyful ending. Thirsty men and starving men came together. Laiton's bread and Scarlet's 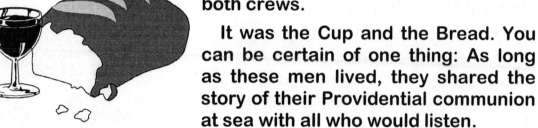 water brought life and hope back to both crews.

It was the Cup and the Bread. You can be certain of one thing: As long as these men lived, they shared the story of their Providential communion at sea with all who would listen.

Questions/Activities

1. Were members of Captain Scarlet's crew sincere in their concern about rescuing the longboat? Where they right or wrong?

> Answer: They were probably very sincere. They didn't want to see Laiton and his crew die, but they thought that to save them might cause them all to be lost on the sea. As for right or wrong, either answer is correct, depending upon the explanation. Young children might say that they were wrong (knowing the outcome), but the men were right in being concerned about their own survival. They, too, wanted to return to their families.

2. Does this mean that there are situations where it is difficult sometimes to sort out what is clearly right from what is clearly wrong? Can you share any examples?

> Answer: Absolutely. Life does not always point us to easy answers or solutions. War would be one example. During war, individuals are ordered to engage in behaviors that they would not do under normal circumstances (such as fire on the enemy). If a soldier refuses to engage in these behaviors, he is in trouble with his superiors.

3. Part of Captain Scarlet's decision to rescue Laiton and his crew seemed to come from faith in an outcome that he could not yet see completely (faith was discussed in the last story). Does this tell us something about Captain Scarlet?

Answer: It says at least three things about Captain Scarlet: He was a compassionate man, he was accustomed to acting on faith and his actions of faith and compassion in the past had produced good results. We call this experience, the one thing that cannot be taught.

4. After the rescue, do you think both crews had more respect for Captain Scarlet?

Answer: Of course. Just perhaps it caused them to act with more empathy and compassion themselves.

5. Do you think Captain Scarlet ever had any trouble finding men to sail with him?

Answer: For the rest of his seagoing years, Captain Samuel Scarlet probably had men standing in line to sail with him.

6. Would you have been proud to have had Captain Samuel Scarlet for your great-great-great-great-grandfather? Why?

Answer: Answers will vary, but most folks, children and adults alike, would appreciate having the compassion and steadfastness of a Samuel Scarlet in their family history.

7. Activity: Summarize

Have the youngsters form into groups of three or four. Give them this question, and have them answer it as a group. Then, share the answers.

Question: In a sentence or two, would you please summarize the point of this story?

Answer: (There can be many answers, and none are wrong.) Compassion is a wonderful quality. There's never a wrong time to do the right thing.

8. Activity: Role-play

Let your group take turns pretending they are in Captain Scarlet's ship when a crew member spies the longboat carrying Captain Laiton and his men. Encourage them to re-enact the discussion aboard the ship as it might have occurred.

9. Activity: Compassion in action

Consider how your group can do something compassionate within your community. Do it, then process it with the group.

        Answer: Some ideas might include:
A. Adopting a homeless dog or cat at the animal shelter.
B. Adopting and supporting a third-world child their own age.
C. Adopting a senior citizen or a nursing home.
D. Assisting with a homeless shelter or food bank.
E. Becoming involved in a wildlife project.

For many more ideas, including specifics on raising funds and support for projects, see *101 Ways to Make Your Classroom Special* by James D. Sutton (see the reference below).

References:

Marshall and Manuel's, *The Light and The Glory* (previously referenced), was also the source for the story of Captain Laiton and Captain Scarlet.

Sutton, J., *101 Ways to Make Your Classroom Special*. Pleasanton, TX: Friendly Oaks Publications, 1999.

The Advantage

Application

This story stresses the value of just a little extra effort.

Prologue

Zig Ziglar, world-class speaker and teacher, loves to share a story about a fellow who was trying to invent a new soft drink. The man worked hard in the lab and in the production and marketing of his new product, a carbonated beverage he called *Four Up*. The product was a flop.

With renewed vigor he tried again. This time he called it *Five Up*. It was a failure also.

But he was not the sort to give in easily. With one massive effort he gave it one more push, introducing his new product, *Six Up*. It flopped, too; he quit.

"If he had only known just how close he came," Zig shares.

It's important to add, however, that effort alone is not the solution to all problems. We can try harder, but if we keep doing the *wrong* things, it's simply not going to work. Ever.

A suitable substitute for effort has never been found. This short story makes a good point.

The Story (The Advantage)

Asports psychologist tells a story about his 10-year-old daughter. This child was born without a muscle in one foot, requiring that she wear a special brace.

One day she came home all excited. "Daddy," she shouted, "we had a field day at school, and I participated."

But before he could respond, his daughter continued. "Daddy, I won *two* events. But I *did* have an advantage."

He figured the girl would explain that she was given a head start in a race, or something similar. But he figured wrong.

"Daddy," she shared jubilantly, her eyes dancing, "I had to *try* harder!"

Questions/Activities

1. Why did the girl consider the fact that she tried harder an advantage?

Answer: This is a very interesting question that probably has more than one answer. Consider that she thought that trying harder was something that few were willing to do. Since she was willing to try harder, it was to her a distinct advantage.

2. Do you believe that trying harder is an advantage?

Answer: Since the word "advantage" refers to some quality or trait that few others have, any sort of advantage in competition would be helpful. Trying harder would then be an advantage, just as size, speed, special knowledge and other qualities would be an advantage.

3. When would trying harder be a strong advantage?

Answer: It would be an especially strong advantage if others were not willing to match the effort.

4. Why would some people not care to try harder?

Answer: Again, there are many answers to the question, but people who were convinced that, regardless of what they did, things were not going to work out, probably wouldn't try harder. They might not even try at all.

5. Would trying harder ever *not* be an advantage?

Answer: This question has at least two answers.
A. Trying harder would not be an advantage if *everyone* was trying harder. (It would be an honorable effort, and even the right thing to do, but it wouldn't be an advantage.) People who advance to higher and higher levels of competition as they are victorious also know that the competition gets tougher and tougher because everyone there is a winner.
B. Trying harder would not be an advantage if a person were doing the wrong things, or if they only put in more effort without wisdom. For instance, trying harder to read the directions on a map wouldn't mean much if a person had the wrong map. And trying harder to take out someone's appendix wouldn't be very successful if there was no knowledge or skill regarding how to do the surgery.

6. Can you think of an example in your own life where you were successful after you made a commitment to try harder? Share it.

Answer: Responses will vary here, but this question should make for some great discussion.

7. Activity: Disabilities and Effort

Put the youngsters into groups and ask them to discuss this question: **Sometimes a person who has a disability tries harder and achieves more than they would have if they had not been disabled. Why is this so?**

> Answer: Again there can be many good answers to this question, but a disability offers a challenge to the individual, a challenge that wouldn't be there otherwise. We need to be challenged along the way.

8. Activity: Luck versus Effort

Let the groups work on this question: **What is the connection between luck and effort?**

> Answer: Some luck is real, but not very permanent. You might find a $100 bill on the ground as you are walking down the street, but don't count on it. The most effective kind of luck has been described as "that special point where opportunity and preparation come together." Of course, preparation contains effort. Without it, the opportunity is wasted.

References:

Zig Ziglar is chairman of the Dallas-based Zig Ziglar Corporation. The *Four Up, Five Up, Six Up* anecdote is included here with his permission.

The source for the story about the the daughter of the psychologist came from program #125 of *Insight* audiomagazine (Niles, IL: Nightingale-Conant Corporation, 1993).

The Dog Days of Oklahoma City

Application

Encouragement helps both the encourager and the encouraged. This story and its activities stress the value of lifting up others.

Prologue

I earned my driver's license at 14 (not something I'd recommend today), and always had a job after that. One of my early jobs was with my hometown radio station. By 15, I was a part-time announcer, working just about all of every weekend. Then the owner of the station, Dr. Ben Parker, did something one day that forever changed my life.

He handed me the key to the station. Call it trust, confidence or whatever, it was not the key, but what it represented, that so affected me. He encouraged me with that simple gesture. He gave me more than a key to a radio station; he gave me the key to comprehending my value to him—and to myself.

Not long ago I came across a story about the great Thomas Edison. In the early development of the light bulb, all the glass shells of the bulbs were created one at a time by skilled glassblowers. It took time and effort to make each one.

One day as a bulb shell was completed, Edison gave it to his helper in the lab, a young boy. He instructed the lad to take the bulb upstairs where the experiments were being conducted. The boy tripped on the staircase, dropping the bulb. It shattered, delaying the work while the craftsman created another one.

When the second bulb was completed, Edison handed it to the boy once again (instead of one of the adults standing nearby). The youngster delivered the bulb safely, and the experiments continued.

It's likely that Edison eventually forgot his gesture of encouragement toward that boy, but I'll bet the boy never forgot. A successful life is anchored to experiences such as these.

Encouragement is a quality of relationships that causes an individual to step outside of self to lift up another. It is a totally selfless act that can create permanent benefit. Frankly, we should do more of it.

What follows is a story about encouragement that should connect easily with young people. Isn't it interesting how we can sometimes relate more easily to animals than to people?

The Story (The Dog Days of Oklahoma)

The April, 1995 bombing of the federal building in Oklahoma City brought us all a look at both extremes of human behavior. On the one hand there was senseless, deliberate violence as the bomber parked a truck full of explosives near the building. When it exploded, the lives of many were taken in an instant. And yet this horrible act was also followed by compassion beyond measure from people all over the world.

But it was not totally a human story. As many will remember, special rescue dogs were brought to the scene to help. With their handlers, these dogs searched the rubble and debris of the explosion for any sign of folks buried underneath.

The dogs had no trouble at all finding people. The problem was that most of the individuals located by the dogs were already dead. Many of these dogs worked hard through a whole shift without finding a single person that was still alive, a survivor.

In order that a dog would not become too discouraged, a handler would sometimes "plant" a person in the debris near the end of the animal's shift so that the dog could find them alive.

It seemed to make a difference to the dog.

Questions/Activities

1. Was it important that the trainers encourage these dogs? Why?

Answer: Yes. Like us, the dogs wanted to feel that what they were doing was important and productive.

2. What do you think would have happened if the trainers had never "planted" a live person?

Answer: The dogs would have become discouraged. Eventually, they might lose interest in their work, or perhaps not even care to do their best.

3. Can people sometimes become discouraged, just like these dogs? Explain.

Answer: Sure they can. When we go for a long stretch without feeling like we are significant or that we have done something helpful, useful or meaningful, it becomes very easy to give up.

4. How can they be encouraged?

Answer: A word of encouragement would help. It can be spoken or written, suggesting that they should continue what they are doing and not give up.

5. Is it possible to encourage others before they become discouraged?

Answer: Yes. Probably the best kind of encouragement is the kind that keeps others from becoming too discouraged.

6. The bombing of the federal building in Oklahoma City was a horrible act of violence. Many people, including small children, died that day. But what followed the bombing also showed us some very good things about people. What were some good things that happened?

Answer: There were wonderful acts of kindness. Volunteers came to help look through the rubble for survivors; much assistance and support was given to folks and their families who were victims of the bombing; churches all over the country had special services in memorial and support of those affected by the bombing.

7. Activity : "I need encouragement."

It's very difficult to offer assistance and encouragement to others when you don't know there's a concern or problem. Spend some time with your group stressing that it is a good thing to be able to say to others, **"I'm going through _____ right now, and it's tough. I would appreciate your support and encouragement."**

8. Activity: "E" Cards

Make up some samples of the "E" Card pictured here ("E" stands for Encouragement). Ask if anyone would like to fill out the top of the card with their name and the concern for which they seek encouragement and support.

Collect the cards and pass them down the aisles, encouraging those who will to write a short note of encouragement, or just their name (every encouragement should be signed). When they are all signed, give the "E" Cards back to the youngsters who filled out the top part.

> **"E" Card**
>
> Name:
>
> Concern:
> _____

9. Activity: Encouragement Sheet

This same thing can also be done by collecting the names and concerns of youngsters in the group and writing their name on sheets of newsprint pad. Tear off the sheets from the pad and fasten them to the board or wall. Hang a pencil or felt-tip marker on a string, and encourage others to write supportive and encouraging comments. Give the youngster the sheet at the end of the day.

Reference:

The source of the story of Edison and the boy is James Newton's book, *Uncommon Friends* (New York: Harcourt Brace, 1987).

Treetop Tag

Application

To examine the value of rest and reflection.

Prologue

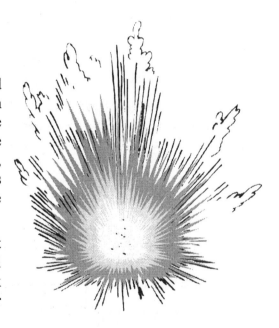

In the late '60s, I was in the Navy stationed with a battalion of marines in DaNang, South Vietnam. We were shelled regularly by the North Vietnamese army. Whenever we came under mortar attack in the middle of the night, the whole compound would spring to life as huge sirens would sound. We'd all head to the underground bunkers for cover.

Before long, 12-hour work shifts on short sleep would take their toll. I learned to bail out of the top bunk, grab my rifle and flack jacket, and race for the bunker without ever really waking up much at all.

Then it happened. One night during the Tet offensive of 1968 we took some heavier than usual shelling. In a deep, exhaustion-induced sleep I scarcely heard the siren. I think I made a feeble attempt to get out of bed, but then I fell back into my bunk. I didn't move. I guess I had made a decision, at least unconsciously, that getting some rest was more important than the best immediate plan for staying alive. I can't remember ever being that tired before or since, but I learned a great deal about the need for rest.

Rest, and the opportunity for silent, still reflection that it affords, aid more than just the body. It refreshes the mind. Consider how one can go to bed frustrated by a problem or concern that they cannot work through, only to awaken with the solution patiently waiting.

There's a passage in the Old Testament that reads: "Be still, and *know* that I am God" (Ps. 46:10). Sometimes the answers come only when we are still enough to take them in.

The Story (Treetop Tag)

Back in the days when survival skills kept the family alive and in one piece, Native-American parents would take their children into the woods and instruct them to sit. They would tell them to sit perfectly still for several hours. They were to listen, observe, absorb and report what they learned when the parents returned for them.

The children said they experienced nothing at first. Gradually, however, the forest began to spring to life. (Of course it had always been alive; they had just become still enough to experience it.) They became aware of the movement of insects and small animals on the forest floor, of birds that would almost touch them, and game of all sort that passed by them. It was a great lesson that the children would use for a lifetime.

I don't live near a forest, but I have taken this lesson into my own backyard. I've cleared my mind enough to focus on everything around me (not always an easy task), from the ant that just crawled across this page to the cardinal that picked up a fallen grape from my vine and carried it up into the oak to share with his mate.

One day my attention was captured by two young squirrels that were playing up high in my magnolia tree. At a frenzied pace they'd play chase, jumping from the large oak to the magnolia, then to the small oak. Then they'd race back across the magnolia to the large oak. It didn't seem to concern them at all that, at that height, a slip would send them crashing into my deck.

As they played, each would, as if on cue, collapse belly-first across the fork of the tree, sides heaving as they paused to catch their breath. Front and back legs dangled limply as they laid across the forks, panting. Then, as if on cue again, the chase was on again. Chasing and resting continued in a cycle that lasted as long as I watched.

Without leaving my own back yard, I had gained two important insights. I learned that one must be still sometimes in order to really see and learn, and I learned that rest is important and necessary.

By-products of Reflection

Insight and solution are often by-products of reflection, those that come to us when we back away from the problem for a bit. In fact, those who knew him well share that the great Thomas Edison used to go fishing without bait, just so he could think without being interrupted.

We've all heard of Thomas Edison's many trials and failures in trying to find just the right element for his electric light bulb. But few have heard of how a cleaning task caused the solution to land right into his lap.

One of the best and simplest elements for the early electric light was plain cotton thread. But the bulb didn't burn long. Edison had put his experiments away one evening and was cleaning the chimneys of the kerosene lamps in his laboratory. Lampblack, carbon from the smoke and soot of the

burning lamps would eventually coat the inside of the chimneys. Dirty chimneys didn't give much light; they had to be cleaned often.

In the midst of this rather mundane chore, Edison realized the value of what he was removing from the chimneys. Carbon was an excellent conductor of electricity. He coated the cotton lightbulb elements with the lampblack. It worked; the new coated element bulbs burned much longer. And the rest, they say, is history.

Sometimes our best ideas come when we *stop* thinking.

Questions/Activities

1. Is rest important? What is the longest you ever went without sleep? What was it like?

Answer: Rest is very important. Most youngsters have never lost a whole night's sleep, but the experiences they share should be interesting.

2. What would happen to a person who went way too long without any rest at all?

Answer: A lot of things, but for sure they stop thinking clearly. Simple cognitive tasks become difficult. After the loss of a lot of sleep, an individual will begin to misperceive and even hallucinate. In other words, they begin to see and respond to things that aren't even there.

3. Someone once said that we lead Space Age lives with Stone Age bodies. What do you think that means? Can it be a problem sometimes? Explain.

Answer: Our bodies are delicate, not always capable of the strain we put them to. A lot of illnesses, such as heart trouble, stroke, ulcers, and even some kinds of cancer can be traced back to excessive stress and strain on the body over the years.

4. Is it possible that some folks could rest too much? What happens then? Discuss this poem:

> *Here lies John Doe;*
>
> *He met the final test.*
>
> *They found him dead upon the couch;*
>
> *He rested himself to death.*

Answer: People who rest all the time are either sick or are trying to avoid something or someone by escaping into rest and sleep. It's not healthy to sleep or rest all the time. The poem is silly in the sense that rest is not lethal, but it is a thought!

5. Do you think that rest and reflection can really help us work out solutions to some of our problems? Can people be so busy trying to "fix" everything that they can't even see the solution?

Answer: Of course. Many products we enjoy today were developed or improved when the inventor was engaged in a different task or activity (such as cleaning the chimneys of the lamps). Some of the best ideas, such as the needle and bobbin of the sewing machine, came to the inventors while they were asleep!

6. A person who doesn't like themselves very much might have some difficulty with a still and quiet activity. Why?

Answer: Who would want to spend time with someone they don't even like?

7. Activity: The Still and Quiet Reflection Log

Encourage your group to follow the directions of the *Still and Quiet Reflection Log* (see the next page). Let them share what they experienced.

Still and Quiet Reflection Log

Date:

Name:

How long did you do this activity?
_____hours _____minutes

What do you remember thinking about?

Did any answers or solutions come to you? Explain.

References:

The story of Edison using the lampblack from the chimneys to coat the filaments is also from James Newton's *Uncommon Friends*.

The "John Doe" poem is this author's.

One-Footed Freedom

Application

This lesson is about dealing with adversity and difficulty. If we can do it well, we might end up stronger than ever.

Prologue

There's an old saying that goes: "The same heat that melts the butter hardens the egg." In other words, everyone is going to encounter some "heat" in their lives. Whether we become better or bitter pretty much depends upon us. Believe me, the world is teeming with examples of both.

I knew a man who once worked as an electrician. In a high-voltage electrical accident, he lost both hands and forearms up to the elbows. He couldn't go back to being an electrician, but he did become very interested in programs, training and jobs for disabled individuals. He became the chief executive officer of a very large organization that employs, trains and finds employment for hundreds of disabled folks. He took an event of extreme adversity and turned it into opportunity, a new and more productive career. And yet there are folks who crumble under the weight of much less. The difference is not the nature of the problem; it's the nature of the person.

But hey, we're not talking only about people. I recall a television program that featured a dog that, through disease and injury, had lost both front and back legs on the same side of her body. She had learned to run behind her master's bicycle, whipping her tail in a circle to maintain balance. It was incredible to watch. I thought of how fortunate the dog was to not know it couldn't be done.

In the following story, another creature, a bird, teaches us a lesson in dealing with adversity.

The Story (One-Footed Freedom)

I didn't notice it at first. She rose so gracefully on the ocean breeze, dipping and calling out with the others for my daughter to toss more bread crumbs.

On the sand, however, she was different from the other seagulls. She hopped strangely, and often flipped out a wing to maintain balance.

She had only one foot.

It was obvious that circumstances didn't slow her down much. She got her share of the bread crumbs and certainly looked well-fed. She could take care of herself, and likely a family as well.

"Katie, that gull is very fortunate," I whispered to my daughter when we made the discovery. "She operates on instinct, driven by a simple, but powerful, message that is etched into her every fiber: SURVIVE."

And that's exactly what she was doing, unburdened by the human qualities of self-pity and bitterness.

When adversity affects people, they not only decide about how they will deal with it, they must decide how they are to interpret its long-term effects upon their lives. Better or bitter; it's a choice.

Mitchell

I know a man who had to make such a choice. His name is Mitchell. He was happily employed as a cable car operator in San Francisco until one day he had an accident on his new motorcycle. He was burned over almost his entire body. Fingers were burned off his hands, and his face was badly burned, requiring many surgeries. He was in the hospital for months, and was in great pain most of the time.

Not long after he recovered from the burns, Mitchell was paralyzed from the waist down while making an emergency landing in his airplane. He could have given up, and few would have blamed him. But he chose to rise above the accidents and the disabilities. He was successful in business, was successful in politics in his home state, and is today a very powerful motivational speaker. He travels the world sharing his story from his wheelchair, encouraging others. Mitchell is fond of saying, "You are not what happens to you; you are what you *do* about what happens to you." It's a choice.

Questions/Activities

1. Did the one-legged gull have a choice? Did she make a decision to do her best with only one leg?

> Answer: Not really. As the story indicates, animals operate on instinct. Instinct is like prepackaged learning that tells an animal what they need to know and do. You don't see puppies and kittens going to school; they don't need to. But instinct is limited. Although it can help a gull survive, it can't help her play the piano.

2. But what if the gull thought like a person, and spent all her time feeling sorry for herself and always thinking of things she couldn't do?

> Answer: For starters, she'd starve to death.

3. People can make choices (decisions). What do their choices say about them?

Answer: They say something about how they feel about themselves, about how they value their decisions and about their confidence in following their choices.

4. Is it sometimes easier to choose to be helpless?

Answer: Of course. It takes the least amount of courage to do nothing.

5. Do you have to lose a leg, or be burned or paralyzed to experience some difficulty and adversity in life?

Answer: No you don't. Most people won't ever have to deal with these kinds of problems. But they might have to deal with failure on a task, the loss of a pet or loved one, a prolonged illness or maybe the divorce of their folks. All of these things and more cause us to have to make decisions about how we will deal with them.

6. Mitchell sometimes shares that he is fortunate because his disability is an obvious one. He notes that the toughest disabilities are those that are not so obvious. What do you think he means?

Answer: People tend to be more understanding of disabilities they can see, such as a person in a wheelchair, or a visually disabled person with a guide dog. They might not be so understanding toward a person with a less obvious disability, such as learning disabilities, hearing difficulties or mental illness. Mitchell might also be saying that we all have disabilities; some just show more than others.

7. Activity: Dr. Frankl's Choice

Dr. Viktor Frankl wrote a wonderful book about choices. It is called *Man's Search For Meaning*. Dr. Frankl was a Jew in Europe during World War II. He lost his home, his family, and almost his life. Daily he dealt with the idea that he might be the next one to be killed in the prison camp; many were killed. And yet, as bad as things were for him, Dr. Frankl said he still had at least one choice that he could make. See if your group might be able to come up with what the choice was.

Answer: Actually, it was the choice of his attitude of how he would handle the experience. Dr. Frankl survived and was freed from the prison camp when the war was over in 1945. He went on to help many, many people.

8. Activity: "Why is it?"
Why is it that, given the exact same adversity and difficulty, there are some people who just handle it much better?

Answer:

A. They, like Mitchell, can separate themselves from what is happening to them.

B. They understand that difficulty and adversity come to everyone sooner or later.

C. They know they are capable of handling it, and perhaps have handled it in the past.

D. They know where to go for help and encouragement.

References:

Read all of W Mitchell's story in his book, *The Man Who Would Not Be Defeated* (Waco, TX: WRS Publishing, 1993). (An interesting note: "W" is his first name, not an initial.)

Frankl, V., *Man's Search for Meaning*. Boston: Beacon Press, 1959.

A Little Push

Application

This lesson is intended to show youngsters the benefits of helping others.

Prologue

Although it's man's nature to be helpful to others, it also seems to be his destiny. Helping others, it seems, helps the helper as much as the helped.

At one time I was the consulting psychologist for a group of young boys who lived in a special group home for emotionally and behaviorally disturbed children. The Christmas season was always especially difficult on them and the staff. They received so many gifts and so much attention that they began to focus only on what they could *get*. Their behavior always worsened.

During a treatment team meeting, a staff member suggested we take the boys on a day-trip to a large homeless shelter in San Antonio. The boys pitched in, doing small chores and helping distribute food and clothing to folks who had nothing. There was an abrupt and positive change in these young men, and the Christmas trip to the homeless shelter became a regular event.

Perhaps the very young can teach us all a powerful lesson in helping. The late Dr. Leo Buscaglia was fond of telling the story about a 4-year-old whose neighbor, an elderly gentleman, had lost his wife. Upon seeing the man crying, the lad went into the neighbor's yard, climbed up into his lap, and sat with him. When his mother asked him what he had said to the man, the little boy replied, "Nothing; I just helped him cry."

This next story is about some help in the form of a little push.

The Story (A Little Push)

The loss of NASCAR legend Dale Earnhardt was most untimely. By his own account, he always regretted dropping out of high school, yet he went on to set records and earned over $41 million in NASCAR racing before his death.

Early on, Earnhardt knew what he wanted to do, he knew he was good at it, and he had a passion to become one of the best. But he also knew the value of having a little help from others along the way. In an interview, he once shared a story that included his father, Ralph Earnhardt, also a race car driver. Dale recalled the only time he was ever on the track in the same race with his dad. It was a Grand National race in 1972.

 Ralph had a comfortable lead in the race. In fact, he was beginning to "lap" the field, meaning that he was so far ahead in the race that he was beginning to pass the slower cars for the second time. Dale, barely more than a teen at the time, was coming up on the third-place car. He attempted to pass, but his opponent wouldn't budge. He tried everything he knew; no luck. As the race neared the finish, Dale figured he would have to settle for a fourth-place finish. Not bad, but he wanted better.

Suddenly, Dale saw his father coming up from behind. Ralph Earnhardt put his bumper against his son's car and, with the younger Earnhardt giving it all one final effort, he pushed Dale into a third-place finish.

That finish remained one of Dale's sweetest victories, made even more memorable by the fact that Ralph Earnhardt died shortly thereafter of a heart attack at 45. They were never to race together again.

Questions/Activities

1. Do you think Dale Earnhardt ever gave someone else a push?

Answer: Probably. Interestingly enough, many believe that Earnhardt died trying to help his teammates. NASCAR racing is usually a team event, with several drivers in the same team on the track at the same time. The team shares the victory of any driver on the team. Near the finish of the race, team members will do all they can do to help their lead car to get and keep their position.

2. But why would people do things that might cost them their lives?

Answer: As long as man has been on this planet, he has often risked his life for a goal or a victory that was important to him. It will probably always be that way.

3. Did you ever get a push, some extra help, from someone at a time when you really needed it? What happened then?

Answer: Answers will vary.

4. Did you ever give a push (some extra help) to someone else? What happened then?

Answer: Again, the answers will vary.

5. In Dr. Buscaglia's story, what does it mean to "help" someone cry?

Answer: It means feeling the sorrow and sadness *with* someone, instead of feeling sorry *for* someone. There's a great difference between the two.

6. Activity: "Thanks for the Push!" coupons.

Make up five copies of the "Thanks for the Push!" coupons for each group member. Ask them to give them to people who help them in a specific way. Make sure they keep a record of to whom and why they give out the coupons. Do this activity for a week, then have a time of sharing.

References:

The source of the Dale Earnhardt story was the 2/28/01 commemorative issue of *Sports Illustrated*.

"Connected"

Application

This lesson explains the concept of interdependence, showing how we are all "connected," and how the actions of one of us affect us all.

Prologue

We live in a complex world that is getting more, not less, complex. Our survival as classmates, families and as a national or global community depends on our ability to work together to accomplish together that which cannot be accomplished alone. If we are able to do this well, it is said that we are interdependent. By definition, teams, such a work or sports teams, are interdependent. This interdependence, this connectedness, is the source of their greatest strength.

Here's a piece of prose that was written by John Donne almost 400 years ago. It well describes how we are all connected in spirit and in life. It is titled, "No Man is an Island."

... No man is an island, entire of itself; every man is a piece of the continent,

a part of the main. If a clod be washed away by the sea, Europe is the less,

as well as if a promontory were, as well as if a manor of thy friend's or of

thine own were. Any man's death diminishes me, because I am involved in

mankind; and therefore never send to know for whom the bell tolls;

it tolls for thee ...

I first read this piece in a high school literature text. I instantly sensed what Mr. Donne was saying. It touched me then; it touches me still.

The following story gives us a literal example of how interdependence works in nature. It's surprising how much we can learn from a few trees.

The Story ("Connected")

Harold is a tree, a strong, healthy tree. He lives along the creekbed in the shadow of the taller trees on top of the knoll.

Even in times of little rain, Harold draws all the moisture he needs from the creek. But what he really needs most sometimes is a bit more sun.

Robert is Harold's tree friend. Robert lives on top of the knoll where the sun is plentiful. But there are times when he could use a little more moisture.

Margaret is also a tree. She grows on the slope of the hill between Harold and Robert. Margaret is pretty content with her station in life. She gets enough sun, although not as much as Robert, and she gets enough moisture, although not as much as Harold.

All three trees do quite well. How is this so?

Fixed by a Fungus

Trees growing close together develop root systems that connect with each other. There is a type of fungus that completes the connection between their roots. Then, as a result of this connection, the trees have the ability to share life-sustaining nutrients with the trees around them. Harold shares moisture with Margaret; Margaret passes it on to Robert. Robert then shares sun nutrients with Margaret, who passes some of them on to Harold.

On this knoll it's more than survival; it's thrival. Each tree takes what it needs and passes on the rest. It's the leafy version of how it should work with people.

Trees are different from people in that they have to grow right where they are planted. They make the best of it. But there's another way that Harold, Margaret and Robert are different from us. They never have headaches or ulcers.

Questions/Activities

1. Why do you think the trees in this story have "people" names?

Answer: Probably so that people will identify with them. Would it have been the same story if the trees were described only as three elms? Probably not. Consider what happens when children bring home a stray dog or cat. They have it named before they bring it into the house.

2. What would happen if one of the three trees decided to keep all the moisture or sunlight for itself?

Answer: First of all, only Margaret could hold back on both because Harold needed sun to stay healthy and Robert needed moisture. But if any of the trees became selfish, it would quickly affect them all.

3. Do people ever behave in selfish ways? What can happen?

Answer: Of course, they do. People who start wars often act selfishly, and we're all familiar with the high price of war. Many animals (and even plants) like the passenger pigeon are now extinct because man was selfish and uncaring. And the same goes for the way we have selfishly harmed our environment, causing things like acid rain and the deterioration of the ozone layer.

4. Share and discuss John Donne's piece, "No Man is an Island." Tie in how, 400 years ago, he discussed this very problem.

5. What are some benefits of being interdependent (connected)?

Answer: There can be many responses to this question. Here are a few:
A. We don't have to know how to do everything. (If you don't believe this is important, just try making your own eyeglasses.)
B. We get to enjoy the company and companionship of others.
C. Families start when a couple gets married; they become interdependent.
D. Working together we can accomplish something we could not do alone, such as build the Hoover Dam.
E. The Pilgrims in story #7 survived only because they were interdependent.

6. Is it possible to be interdependent with people we don't even know?

Answer: It happens all the time. Ever fly on an airplane? Did you know the pilot and crew? Yet you trusted them to safely take you where you wanted to go. And the pilot and crew trusted that you and the other passengers would buy enough tickets so that they would have jobs. That's interdependence. Also consider the interdependence in your own future family, your children and grandchildren. You don't know them yet, but they are very, very real.

7. Activity: The Three Trees

Take turns letting five youngsters develop a short skit about the three trees and how they exercise interdependence. Add two more players: the creek and the sun. The sun gives it nutrients (rays) to the tree on the knoll, that takes what it needs and passes on the rest. The creek starts the same cycle with the moisture it provides to the tree growing near its bank. After the group demonstrates interdependence, have them act out what it might be like if even one tree became selfish.

References:

"No Man is an Island" is from *Norton Anthology of English Literature*, fifth edition. New York: W.W. Norton, 1962. Vol 1., 1107.

"Connected," the story of the three trees was told in a sermon by Rev. Charles L. Woodward, pastor of Trinity Baptist Church in Pleasanton, Texas.

The "Problem" with Happiness

Application

This story and its questions and activities are intended to challenge one to think about the true nature of happiness.

Prologue

Back in the late summer of 1998, I was privileged to hear Dr. Anthony Campolo, a Baptist minister, speak on the topic of happiness. I'd have to say that he didn't change my thinking on the subject, but he did affirm my thoughts.

Dr. Campolo comes from a strong Italian-American background, people who approach happiness differently than most folks. Different families, especially families with distinctly different heritage, desire different things for their children. Dr. Campolo suggests that if you ask Asian-American parents what they want for their children, they will often say that they want their children to be successful. And, more often than not, that's exactly what happens.

If you ask Italian-American parents what they want for their children, Dr. Campolo suggests that they will say, "We want them to be good." Although "good" lends itself to some pretty wide interpretations, it does suggest appropriateness of behavior and relationships. But he notes that if you ask most American parents about their heartfelt desires for their children, they will usually say, "We want them to be happy."

The problem is, how do you define happiness? It's pretty vague (and "vague" is usually unattainable). Dr. Campolo suggests that those who make it their objective to chase after happiness might well be the most selfish and self-aggrandizing folks here on planet Earth. And there's another characteristic common in these folks: They are *not* happy. Their lives and relationships show it.

This story looks closely at what happiness is—and what it is not.

The Story (*The "Problem" with Happiness*)

As a kid growing up in Abilene, I attended Vacation Bible School every summer. For some reason, I was really good at memorizing Bible verses. To this day, I recall how I disagreed with Solomon, a leader known for his great wisdom (a pretty brash move for an 8-year-old). He wrote this classic Proverb:

> *A good name is rather to be chosen than great riches.*
>
> —Proverbs 22:1 KJV

"Just give me the riches," I said, "and I won't care *what* you call me." I was very wrong, of course. Wealth and material possessions have little to do with lasting happiness or the sort of character that will hold firm when everything else doesn't. And as I grew older, I realized that it is my name and the reputation attached to it that will last long after I am gone.

So, if happiness is not being totally immersed in the "good life," then what is it? Well, for starters it appears that those who are truly happy don't chase after it. It comes to them. Dennis Prager, author of *Happiness is a Serious Problem*, suggests that real happiness is difficult to define. (By the way, his book tells us that happiness itself is not a problem, but rather the way in which some folks try to capture it.)

If this is the case, then just how could Mr. Prager write a whole book about happiness? Very simple; just about everyone knows what *unhappiness* is. Some thoughts on happiness:

Happiness is NOT financial success. Mr. Prager suggests that just the opposite is usually true. The wealthy are often more miserable than the non-wealthy. This is not to say that wealth makes folks miserable, but rather a focus on wealth and what it can buy. Wealthy folks who are quite happy realize that their wealth is only a resource, a tool. They have decided to use it rather than having it use them. For them, giving part of their wealth away or putting it to good use for others are prime sources of their happiness.

Happiness is NOT perpetual pleasure. Too often, pleasure is confused for happiness. There's more to it than that. Robin Sedgwick and her husband Richard are dear family friends of ours (our son claims her as his *second* mother). Their family pet, a Scottie named McGregor, became very sick. The only compassionate solution to his pain was to "put him down." (Isn't it interesting how we develop vocabulary to soften the blow, even for a pet?)

Robin did something I've never had the courage to do. She held McGregor tightly in her arms as the vet administered the injection. Then she continued to hold him.

Was she having fun? I seriously doubt it. Did she do the right thing? Of course (it was the right thing for her to do at that moment, and she knew it). Does doing the right thing contribute to Robin's happiness? Of course.

Happiness IS gratitude and faithfulness. A grateful heart always extends outward—even to a dying dog. Faithfulness, the other component of a happy heart, is measured by how we honor our commitments, our relationships, and our most closely held principles.

Someone reportedly asked Mother Teresa why she worked so hard to save and serve the sick, starving and dying in Calcutta. It seemed that her efforts were so slight compared to the depth of the need. She quickly responded with: "I was not called to do perfect service. I was called to be faithful."

And if that's not a Proverb, perhaps it ought to be.

———————————

Questions/Activities

1. Was what Robin did for her dog something that every pet owner should do?

Answer: The quick answer to this question might be "Yes," but the real answer is deeper (as real answers usually are). As the story indicates, it was the right thing for Robin to do. For her not to have held the dog would have been wrong for her. It would not necessarily be wrong for someone else.

2. Benjamin Franklin said: "The Constitution only provides for the *pursuit* of happiness. You must catch it for yourself." What do you think he meant by that?

Answer: It means no one can hand your happiness to you. It takes some work on your part.

3. In his book, *Happiness is a Serious Problem*, Mr. Prager quotes a lady (Helen Telushkin) who said, "The only happy people I know are people I don't know well." What do you think she meant by that?

Answer: When we really know someone well, we generally know all of the ups and downs of that person. On the other hand, we tend to see strangers as not having a care in the world. Of course, that's rarely true.

4. I know a man who went to Calcutta and worked with Mother Teresa and the Missionaries of Charity. He shared that she asked him not to stay there, but to go back and serve in the most impoverished nation in the world—the United States of America. Since we're one of the richest countries in the world, what do you think she meant?

Answer: There are many ways to be impoverished—but for starters she probably meant that we have a lot of growing to do in this country with regard to morality, spirituality, relationships and a willingness to reach deep to help others.

5. Do you believe that gratitude is a part of happiness? If that's so, how can we exercise more gratitude?

Answer: By first noticing what others have done for us in the past and what they continue to do for us. Then it is important to find ways to express our gratitude to them.

6. Activity: "How would you *really* know?"

Break up into groups and issue this question: "How would you know that a wealthy person was really happy?" (It would probably be helpful to first let the youngsters identify celebrities, athletes or community figures who are known to be wealthy.)

Answer: We need to be cautious with this question so that we don't infer that there is anything wrong with being wealthy. Really wealthy folks, however, would be happy with or without their wealth. This thought leads us to consider at least three questions:

1. Were they happy before they became wealthy?

2. Could they be still be happy if they were to lose their wealth? (In other words, what would happen if the wealth was taken away?)

3. Do they use part of their wealth to help others in some way?

References:

When I heard him, Dr. Anthony Campolo was a keynote speaker at the annual convention of the *National Speakers Association* in July of 1998 in Philadelphia.

Prager, D., *Happiness is a Serious Problem*. New York: HarperCollins, 1998.

Check Your Spirit Pail

Application

This section is best used with groups. It helps explain how even the best of intentions toward others can blow up in our faces. How we deal with this sort of rejection can say a lot about our character, and it can better prepare us for "next time."

Prologue

In the work and mission of *Alcoholics Anonymous*, three words are used to describe the disease of alcoholism: cunning, baffling and powerful. This disease is so cunning, so baffling and so powerful that I have seen excellent and committed addiction counselors with years of sobriety relapse and fall all the way to the bottom. It is so cunning, so baffling and so powerful that I knew of one alcoholic who, upon leaving a program of treatment in the hospital, changed his ticket at the airport. He left his wife and family to travel across the country to take up with someone he had met in treatment.

Compulsive disorders and conditions, like overeating, gambling, hypochondriasis and workaholism are, at their core, no different really than addictions to drugs and alcohol. This has been validated in research.

It has been said that compulsive disorders represent the only disease (addiction) where the patient struggles desperately to *stay* sick. Dysfunctional individuals create dysfunctional families, which create dysfunctional children.

Compulsive disorders are, indeed, cunning, baffling and powerful. Whenever we attempt to help a dysfunctional adult, family or child, we do battle with an awesome force. Quickly, the struggle can cause us to feel ineffective, powerless and discouraged, especially when it spits in the face of our sincerest intentions. It hurts when you're seen as "the enemy" by someone you are trying so hard to help.

This story first appeared in my book, *It Makes a Difference*, and speaks to these concerns.

The Story (*Check Your Spirit Pail*)

Basically, young people present a number of physical similarities to adults. They come with the basic compliment of two arms, two legs, eyes, ears and all the essential stuff that network all the hardware to a command center we call a brain. The brain operates the machinery.

Most of this machinery is pretty obvious, even to the most casual observer. If a youngster ever came to school missing an arm or leg, chances are that a teacher would not only recognize the loss, but would attempt to do something to make the day a bit easier for that child. This behavior is called empathy and caring.

It was probably invented by a teacher.

What we can't see, however, can affect our ability to understand, let alone empathize. We can't see a youngster's sense of insecurity, fear, apprehension, rage, loss, shame or loneliness. We can only observe the machinery. These affects, these feelings, attach themselves to thoughts, eventually influencing the deterioration of the whole system.

Sometimes the equipment works pretty well, with only an occasional knock or ping. There is no emergency. The machinery keeps on running, though perhaps not at its best. But that's okay; life can be like that from time to time.

There are those times, however, when the equipment malfunctions. It still works, but just barely. Even extra rest and nourishment are barely enough to just "get by." In fact, too much sleep and too much food create even more problems. This youngster seems to exist in a state of perpetual deficiency. What is missing?

What is missing is not the fuel of rest. Nor is it the fuel of nourishment. What's missing is the fuel of spirit. The fuel of spirit lends purpose; purpose keeps the machinery going.

When the fuel of spirit is lost, misplaced or allowed to drain carelessly onto the ground, the machinery is affected. It can either respond to the loss, or it can react to it. Let's consider reaction first.

If it *reacts* to a lack of spirit fuel, the machinery can become upset, vengeful, even violent. It can attempt to run down and destroy anyone who would so thoughtlessly cause it to starve. Since rage hampers both reasoning and vision, this angry machine might try to run over everything and everyone in its path. It will even run over someone approaching it with a pail full of refreshing spirit.

Command Central, the brain that pulls the levers and operates the controls, can attempt to find something else, a spirit substitute, for the fuel it so desperately seeks. So it fills its tanks with fleeting "feel goods" of instant pleasure and activity, hoping the equipment will be revived and return to its working state.

But the "feel good" fuel is a poison in disguise. It destroys everything, and it doesn't take long to finish the job.

When the machinery *responds* to a lack of spirit fuel, it is usually not driven to harm others, even though it is so needy. Spirit depletion may move it in one of two directions. It might, for instance, isolate itself and accept the notion that no fuel is ever coming. Eventually, the machinery comes to a complete stop.

It dies.

Or Command Central might scan its memory of spirit fuel sources in the past and search out the replenishment it needs. It resolves to leave no pail unsearched. It warmly considers all offers. But it is not fooled; it searches only for the real thing.

Folks who are successful components of the helping profession, such as educators and counselors, generally have plenty of spirit fuel to operate their own equipment. In fact many of them carry this spirit fuel well in excess of what they need for themselves.

Some actually manufacture the stuff! They not only have plenty of this kind of fuel to give away, they are absorbed in the process of, pail in hand, searching out machinery in need of a long overdue fill-up.

These folks are not only successful most of the time, they are very necessary. They are often overworked and underpaid. Their contributions, however, can never be minimized. They find machinery headed for the scrap heap and send it back to work.

But sometimes they are fooled. They approach machinery that obviously needs a transfusion of spirit, but, just as they begin to offer support, the frightened or angry machinery tries to run them over! Or, when their back is turned, the machinery tries to steal their spirit pail.

They are deeply hurt and confused. Many times they become very angry at the pitiful machine that they were only trying to help. Then they are angry some more, sometimes at themselves. "It doesn't make sense. We try to help others only to have them hurt us," they say. They may wonder if it really makes a difference to keep on trying to even help at all. Some, but only a few, toss their spirit pails in the corner of the garage and leave them there.

They quit. "It's just not worth the effort or the pain," they say in disgust.

But those that don't quit try to learn something from the hurt, the anger and the confusion. They learn how not to get run over while offering help. They learn how to protect themselves from thieves. They learn how to be sensitive and vulnerable without becoming a hostage. They learn how to be balanced and happy, and they learn to share with others that true happiness is much more than just the pleasure of the moment. They learn how to live, how to share and how to teach that happiness is victory.

Questions/Activities

1. This story suggests that a person can have their needs met for rest and nourishment, and still be very needy. What is this missing "ingredient"?

   Answer: It is spirit.

2. Activity: The Meaning of Spirit

   Look up the definitions of **"spirit"** and **"spiritual."** Discuss the semantic meanings for the words as well as what they mean to individuals in the group.

3. How important is it for a person to recognize the importance of spirit in their lives?

   Answer: Spirit is tied to purpose and hope. Returning prisoners of war, for example, have shared that these qualities were the ones that most helped them to survive.

4. Activity: The Difference

Put the youngsters in groups and have them brainstorm the difference between "spirit" and "religion," or "spiritual" and "religious."

Answer: There is significant difference. A spiritual person subscribes to an unseen positive force in their life that gives them direction, purpose, hope and strength. A religious person typically affiliates with a denomination, group or sect of individuals who share a set of beliefs about how the spirit operates, and how they are to respond to it in accordance with their beliefs and their trust and faith in those beliefs. As a point of contrast, the early explorers found the Native Americans Indians to be deeply spiritual people, although they were not, for instance, of any Protestant, Catholic or Jewish religion.

5. Activity: Why?

Have the groups brainstorm this question: **The story suggests that sometimes those who are very needy might either refuse the help of others, or even attempt to do them harm. Why?**

Answer: All reasonable answers are acceptable. Here are three:
A. **Denial**—A needy individual might invest a considerable amount of effort and energy into believing that a problem simply doesn't exist. Someone offering help to this individual is, by the nature of their offer, implying that there is a problem. Help is refused as a way of maintaining the denial. (Minimization is a close cousin to denial. A minimizing person might say that, even if there is a problem, "It's not *that* bad; I don't need any help with it.")
B. **Trust**—By history, the person might not have any experience of ever believing that someone might just want to help them (with no strings or conditions.
C. **Fear**—Fear is the greatest immobilizer of them all. Feelings and responses of fear stem from a sense that one has low worth or value, and incapable of an appropriate response.

6. Activity: What Can We Do?

Have the groups brainstorm this question: **What are some things that a person can do if they really want to help others, but do not wish to be discouraged or hurt?**

Answer: It's a challenge. There are never any guarantees against being hurt or rejected, but giving up doesn't seem to be the answer either.

For starters, it is important to look at our motivation for wanting to help others. Those who have a "hidden" agenda might be trying to do the right things for the wrong reasons. Their gestures of help and assistance might be designed to convince themselves and others of their goodness and decency. Whenever they are turned away, or their help is rejected, they feel attacked at the level of their own self-esteem.

This is not to say that the rejection of one's good intentions isn't painful. It's just that healthy folks are more successful keeping it in perspective. Someone once said that the secret to a full and happy life is to be centered in one's ability to do good work, to perform generous deeds, and to have grateful thoughts. Such an individual has knowledge of their own worth, and is comfortable with it. They can genuinely offer their help and support to others without being damaged by the negative outcome of a decent gesture.

Reference:

Sutton, J., *It Makes a Difference*. Pleasanton, TX: Friendly Oaks Publications, 1990. (Reprinted with permission.)

This story, "Check Your Spirit Pail," appeared in the original *Windows*.

Fowl Play

Application

This story should stimulate some spirited discussion within your group. It speaks to the value of spontaneity and play to the human condition.

Prologue

As the old Mac Davis song goes: "You've gotta stop and smell the roses." Good song; great advice.

As I was considering this very concept while driving between Burnet and Lampasas (Texas), I suddenly was overwhelmed by a barrage of red, yellow and purple on the side of the highway. Texas wildflowers.

I took Mac's advice, pulled my car over to the side of the road, and paused to take them in. They weren't roses, but they weren't bad.

As I see it, the concept here has two components. One is the idea of the need for rest and relaxation, and the other is spontaneity, an invigorating diversion from what threatens to trap us in a world that only operates in black and white. I'm speaking of the sort of spontaneity that is an explosion of color on the big screen. It might not be a requirement for remaining alive, but it's pretty important for real and lasting joy.

Just the process of resting helps us to reframe things. It is no coincidence that our best thinking and most creative moments come when our focus is more on rest than work (the topic of another story in this book). Dan Burrus, author of *TechnoTrends*, is fond of saying that we hardly ever do anything creative in our offices. Good point.

Spontaneity is associated with the process of being "real," and feeling comfortable about it. As a human quality, it is directly connected to one's self-esteem and the willingness to take a risk. A lack of spontaneity might be demonstrated by a person who must overcontrol everything (and everyone) in and around their life. This person doesn't allow themselves to ever have fun because "fun" is silly, and silly means foolish and bad.

To emotionally healthy folks, spontaneity is walking in the rain, flying a kite and squishing barefoot through the mud. It can even be the act of sneaking into work with a water pistol and squirting the boss. (Try that thought on for size!)

This story will hopefully capture the flavor of spontaneity. Incidentally, I do understand that the word "fowl" is usually reserved for birds that might wind up on the dining room table (chicken, turkey, duck), but I liked the title. I also "spontaneously" stayed with the picture of a male cardinal below, although the story is about a *female* redbird.

The Story (*Fowl Play*)

One morning while feeling particularly overwhelmed with preparations for a series of speaking engagements, I paused to turn the lawn sprinkler on in the back yard. As a mist covered the fence, a female cardinal settled on one of the dog-eared cedar pickets.

She was having a grand time, apparently unaware of my presence. She faced the fine spray of the sprinkler, ruffling her feathers to let the droplets bathe her. She then hopped from one picket to the next, allowing the water to reach her wings, back and tail. She then turned around and hopped back to her original spot to bathe her other side, pausing once to clean her beak against a picket.

"Sure must be nice to have the luxury of being so spontaneous," I said to myself. "If she and her friends had any *real* problems (like mine!), they wouldn't waste their time jumping around in the sprinkler."

Not that I had never played in the sprinkler. My sister and I spent many summer afternoons running through the sprinkler and playing on the damp Bermuda grass. But that was during our growing-up years in Abilene. And it was a long time ago.

I concentrated on standing stone-still so that I would not startle her. I wondered what her agenda was for the day. I was pretty sure it didn't include romping around in the water sprinkler all morning. Sooner or later, she would have to break away to take care of other things.

What other things? Things like trying to feed a family? Things like surviving whatever the weather brings? Things like having to keep an eye out for the kid with the new BB gun down the street, or the neighbor's cat? Things like wondering what to do if the roofers cut away the branch that holds her nest? Things like dealing with all kinds of bird problems.

Few are exempt from the rigors of life—not even redbirds. But perhaps a moment or two in the sprinkler helps.

Almost as suddenly as she had arrived, the lady turned and took to the air. She skillfully navigated the power lines and zoomed up and over the oak tree.

"Thanks," I whispered as she quickly left my sight.

"You're quite welcome," a soft voice seemed to answer back.

Questions/Activities

The whole concept of spontaneity is rather abstract. Even though young children demonstrate it better than adults, they may have difficulty talking about it. For them, the concepts and terms will need to be made concrete. For example, they might understand spontaneity as: "Doing something good or fun without planning it or thinking much about it first."

1. After sharing this story, write the word "spontaneity." Ask the youngsters to write down what they think it means.

2. After a bit of discussion, have a member of the group look up "spontaneity" or "spontaneous" in the dictionary. Discuss its meaning.

3. Read the story again and ask, "Who was spontaneous in this story?"

Answer: The redbird (cardinal), of course.

4. What did the redbird do that was spontaneous?

Answer: She played in the water from the sprinkler.

5. Was the redbird spontaneous because she didn't have anything to worry about?

Answer: No.

6. What did the story mention as some of the redbird's worries?

Answer: The weather, the neighbor's cat, the boy with the BB gun, feeding her family and the roofers.

7. As a contrast to the risk of being spontaneous, ask your group to consider the worries or problems that any animal might have.

8. Activity: Have your groups brainstorm ways that they have seen other animals being spontaneous. Share these.

9. Can people be spontaneous?

Answer: Of course.

10. Activity: Have your groups make lists of spontaneous things people can do.

Answer:
A. Like the redbird, play in the water sprinkler.
B. Play with water guns.
C. Sing a song.
D. Spin a yo-yo.
E. Do a cartwheel.
F. Walk barefoot in the mud or on a beach.
G. Build a kite.
H. Fly a kite.
I. Make mud pies.
J. Eat mud pies!
K. Make a sand castle.
L. Learn to juggle.
M. Do a magic trick.

11. Are animals more spontaneous than humans? Why?

Answer: Probably, because much of their behavior is instinctual. Instinct helps them live and behave automatically. Humans do not have much instinct, but they are capable of learning more than animals—much more. If you don't believe it, try to teach your cat to juggle! The one disadvantage humans have is that they are more capable of making poorer decisions than animals. Over time, this can cause them (humans) to become fearful of trying to be spontaneous.

12. Are children more spontaneous than adults? Why or why not?

Answer: Of course they are! They have not yet learned how *not* to be spontaneous.

13. Are children more spontaneous than animals?

Answer: Who knows?

14. Is it possible for someone to spontaneously do the *wrong* thing?

Answer: Not really. By definition, spontaneity is the *right* thing. Doing the wrong thing would be more descriptive of something called "impulsivity."

15. How would you define impulsivity? What would be some examples?

Answer: Any behaviors that are done quickly without much thought or planning, but which would only serve to hurt or endanger self or others in some way would be an example of impulsivity.

> Answer: Examples might include:
> A. Physically provocative behavior.
> B. Saying hurtful things to others.
> C. Someone spending all their money on something they want, only to be broke for a long time.
> D. Someone getting angry and quitting their job without having another job to go to.
> E. Buying a new car with no sure way to keep up the payments.

16. If impulsive behavior is so bad, why do people ever engage in it?

> Answer: This kind of behavior is often associated with a condition called "compulsivity." It its severest form, it becomes a "compulsive disorder," which is like a type of addiction (it was discussed in the prologue of the last story).

Reference:

Burrus, D., *Technotrends*. New York: HarperBusiness, 1993.

This story, "Fowl Play," was part of the orginal *Windows*.

I'd Rather Have Pizza

Application

This section addresses the fact that we all need nurturance and affirmation in our lives. To the degree that we might expect these things from those who cannot give them, we are vulnerable to frustration and feelings of emptiness.

Prologue

Eleven years ago, my children were still living at home, very much involved in high school. Occasionally, I would take a morning off during the week to sleep in and recharge my batteries. With my wife at work and my son and daughter off to school, I had the place to myself.

Well ... *almost* to myself. My sleep and solitude were usually interrupted by a visitor, my daughter's young Lhasa Apso. Her delight in discovering that she had company in the house for a few hours was evidenced by her bright eyes and wagging tail, not to mention the damp collection of doggy toys that she had carried up the stairs to deposit in the bed next to me as I slept. (She's still around. In fact, she's sleeping under my chair as I write this. Although she's mostly blind and moves a little slower now, her spirit has never been younger.)

For the morning, her entire agenda was always to please me. She wanted to go wherever I went and do whatever I did. She desired to be totally and completely absorbed into my reality. And she's that way still.

Which is pretty appropriate behavior, I suppose—for a dog. A person behaving in similar ways might be quite sick. Unlike our canine (and feline) friends, healthy humans must constantly balance their dependence upon others with the development of an identity and an autonomy that is uniquely theirs. It's not just important; it's critical.

Youngsters who lack a functional identity of their own feel they must attach themselves to others in order to be "complete." To them, each significant other represents a mirror in which they can observe their reflection. Whenever the mirror is removed, the resulting feelings of uneasiness and anxiety can be overwhelming.

This dependency is made worse when the significant other degrades or depreciates the youngster instead of nurturing and affirming them. Even though such a youngster is likely to be reeling from the hurt of rejection, he or she is driven to go back again and again. They expect things to change, to be different "next time."

But things rarely change.

This story, applicable to both individual and group settings, provides insight into this dynamic. I wrote it for a 16-year-old girl who, one day in group therapy, spoke of her relationship with her mother. I explained the relationship in terms of a metaphor she knew well—her favorite food.

The Story (*"I'd Rather Have Pizza"*)

I love to eat pizza. I could eat pizza for breakfast, lunch and dinner. Just the smell of steaming pepperoni and melted cheese makes my taste buds go crazy.

Sometimes my friends think I like pizza too much. "Try some other things," they say to me. "There are hundreds of good dishes out there," they exclaim. Sometimes I try them. Chow mein with eggroll was nice. Fajitas were tasty. A bacon double cheeseburger was filling.

But I'd rather have pizza.

I've discovered that sometimes eating slice after slice of my favorite pizza does take my mind off some of my problems for awhile. I'm afraid, however, that I will weigh 400 pounds before I run out of problems. I need to change the way I do some things, but I'm scared. But I'm too scared to let things stay the same.

My biggest problem is my mother. Well, not exactly my mother so much, but rather my relationship with her. Sometimes she makes me feel very small and insignificant. Even though I'm 16, I wish that she would just put her arms around me and hold me like a tiny baby. If she could just pat me on the back sometimes, or tell me that, once in a while, I make good decisions, I think my heart would feel satisfied. But I'm beginning to believe that that kind of a relationship with her is a dream that may never come true. In my mind I know this is true, because I can't live at home anymore. I live in a group home with other youngsters like me.

I am fortunate to have peers and adult friends who do understand. They listen to me. They even pat me on the back and tell me when I make good decisions. They help me. They help me a lot.

But I'd rather get these things from my mother.

Then one day, I guess it was a week or so ago, I made a discovery. I discovered something in a place I don't visit very often. I discovered something in my mind.

Here's my discovery. Everyone has special needs. They are like a type of hunger. When others help him or her with that special need, they feed the hunger. Then he or she isn't hungry anymore. But sometimes that hunger, that special need, just lies there aching in a corner of a person's heart. If it's not reached, it just gets hungrier and hungrier. That special need starves.

There's no doubt about it; my mother is my first choice of food for my deepest, most hungry special need. That's right, my mom is like a pizza. But instead of satisfying my hunger, this pizza usually hurts me, leaving me with even deeper and hungrier special needs. It's a pizza that looks great. It even smells great. But arsenic is sprinkled all over it.

That's right; it's a poison pizza.

At the ripe old age of 16, I have a decision to make. I can keep on eating a poison pizza, or I can try other foods to get my needs met. If I eat the pizza, I know I will get sicker and sicker. I could even die. If I try some other foods, which means to turn to others with my deepest, hungriest special needs, I will need to take a risk. Some of those foods might make me sick, but I know that most of them will satisfy my hunger very well. In my head I know that all of this is true, but my heart has trouble believing it.

And there are a lot of foods around. I work in the office for one period a day at school. The principal is very nice to me. He trusts me and gives me responsibility. He tells me when I do a good job. He is so stable and supportive. To me, he's like a thick steak with mashed potatoes. A person could grow strong on a meal like that.

My typing teacher is so sweet. She reminds me of a stack of buttermilk pancakes, with lots of butter and tons of syrup. A boy in my algebra class knows how to make me laugh. It's not a "tee-hee" shallow kind of laugh that starts and stops in the back of my throat, but a deep, soul-cleansing laugh that starts at my toenails and works its way up. He is very tall and very thin, kind of like a French fry. Yes, for some of my special needs, he's a whole family order of fries.

My friends are like ice cream cones. Some are strawberry, while others are chocolate. Some are my very favorite: French Vanilla.

My minister, who counsels with me sometimes, is a big man. He is the kindest person I know. In my life, he's the bacon double cheeseburger, with extra pickles.

I have a new decision to make. If I could never eat pizza again, can I learn to be happy and have joy in my life? With so many other good foods around, I think I can. I'll take that risk.

But I'd *still* rather have pizza.

Questions & Activities

1. Why is the girl in this story so upset and frustrated?

Answer: Because she is hurt and resentful toward her mother.

2. What does she want from her mother?

Answer: She probably wants her mother to stop doing and saying things that cause her to feel so small and insignificant. She also wants her to sometimes pat her on the back and tell her that she is lovable and capable.

3. Will her mother ever do or say those kinds of things?

Answer: Not unless she has some help with it. The girl's mother has probably not had much experience feeling lovable and capable in her own life. How can she give away something she never had?

4. If the mother's response is always the same, why does the girl keep going back to her?

Answer: Her hope is that things will be different "next time," so she keeps on trying and keeps on calling her mother on the phone.

5. In this story, the girl's overattachment to her mother's moods and actions are compared to what?

Answer: The girl's fondness for eating pizza.

6. What does the girl "discover" in her mind?

Answer: She discovers that everyone has special needs, and that these needs are like a special type of hunger.

7. Why was it difficult for the girl to stop eating the poison pizza?

Answer: Because she so deeply wanted her relationship with her mother to be different. She lived with a dim hope that things would be different "next time."

8. What decision did the girl make?

Answer: That she would try other foods to help her with her special needs.

9. Activity: "Hungers" (special needs)

Discuss with your group other kinds of special needs and "hungers" that humans can have.

Answer: A few of these could include needs for:
A. Security
B. Order
C. Belonging
D. Approval
E. Worth
F. Stimulation
G. Growth
(Many of these needs have been discussed in other parts of this book.)

10. Activity: Examples

Have the group examine each one of these needs, further defining examples of it and why it is so important to have the need met.

11. Activity: Experiences

This might naturally lead to a discussion of such things as the divorce of parents or even a death in the family. Tie these losses into the search for others who can help with special needs.

Reference:

This story, "I'd Rather Have Pizza," appeared in the orginal publication of *Windows*.

The Carpet in My Parlor

Application

This story is written in metaphor to help youngsters understand issues of sexual abuse. Aside from the rather obvious use of this story with a child who has been abused (including the residual effects of the trauma), this story is useful in helping any youngster deal with a "secret" they may be keeping from their folks (such as pregnancy or misuse of drugs or alcohol).

Another application is with an entire class or counseling group. The objective in this case would be the development of understanding and empathy toward a peer going through physical, sexual or emotional abuse.

Prologue

I don't know many folks who feel comfortable learning or teaching about sexual abuse of children. As a topic, there is just no way to dress it up and make it smell nice.

The child who has been abused sexually is generally flooded with a number of emotions. The youngster is angry (even rageful) at the abuser and, sometimes, at a caretaker who might have prevented the abuse in the first place. The youngster feels violated and often responsible, resulting in a deep sense of shame. In my opinion, the shame is the most damaging residue of the abuse. It is often more destuctive than the abuse itself.

The sexually abused child is fearful of telling anyone about the abuse. In addition to the abuser's urgings, threats and bribes for the child's silence, the youngster is fearful they would not be believed if they did make an outcry. So they often do nothing.

Sooner or later, the child who is doing nothing winds up in big trouble.

All of these characteristics closely described the 9-year-old that was brought to my office by her mother. She had been abused by a 16-year-old relative. The thing that brought her to treatment, however, was her difficulty in school. As is usually the case, the *real* issue was much more than difficulty with school behavior and academics. She had told her mother about the abuse, but neither one of them were dealing with it very well.

In my work with children, I have been successful using therapeutic stories written in metaphor. I wrote this one specifically for her. When I later read the completed story to her, the tears trickling down her cheeks told me she understood it well.

"Is that kind of how it was?" I asked her.

"Exactly," was her reply.

The questions following the story conclude with a look at the difference between guilt and shame. I didn't really understand the difference until I was in my mid-40s. John Bradshaw managed to explain it to me in such a way that it finally stuck. What a benefit it would be for youngsters to learn these concepts early on in life.

The Story (The Carpet in My Parlor)

Once, I lived in a wonderful house. I helped to keep it beautiful by taking care of the parlor. It was a wonderful room, filled with the finest antique furniture. I enjoyed keeping it nice, and I enjoyed spending time there with my family and my friends.

One day we bought a beautiful carpet for that parlor. It was snow white and very soft. I loved to walk on it barefoot. I enjoyed feeling the deep pile against my toes. I loved that carpet; I loved to clean and vacuum it every day. My family told me how pleased they were with me and the way that I kept the carpet and the parlor looking so nice.

Then one day someone ran through the parlor to get to the other rooms. His feet were caked with dirt and mud. He left huge soiled spots across my beautiful carpet. He wasn't trying to be ugly or mean; he just wanted to go through the parlor quickly. He never stopped to think how important that carpet was to me.

When I first saw the mud stains on the carpet, I wanted to run away. How could I ever tell my mother that I let this horrible thing happen? Even though I knew the soiled carpet was not my fault, somehow I felt responsible.

"Maybe I could fix it," I thought. Maybe it was not so dirty after all. I started to clean some of the smaller spots; the dirt and mud came up! There was a big spot in the middle, however, that would not come clean. I scrubbed, I scraped and I cried, but it was still there. I decided to try to hide it by putting a small rug over the spot.

My mother thought it was strange for me to cover a beautiful carpet with a plain piece of rug, but she didn't say anything. I didn't want to tell her about the spot under the rug because I was afraid that she would be angry at me.

I still got lots of compliments about the parlor and the carpet, but I felt like a knife was poking my heart every time they admired the carpet. "If you only knew about the rug," I would think.

I found myself having trouble at school. For no reason, in the middle of class, I would start thinking about that carpet. Sometimes I would think so hard about it that I even would forget that I was at school. Sometimes I would get behind in my work, or even miss words on the spelling test. I didn't tell my teacher why I was having trouble thinking at school. I didn't tell anyone.

I felt awful keeping this secret. The worst part was not telling my mother about the carpet because we never kept secrets between us. I decided that somehow, some way, I must tell her.

When I took the rug away and showed the spot to my mother, she cried. She said that she was not angry at me, but that she was very upset that I worried so much and so long about the parlor and the carpet. She told me that she had known that something was wrong. She said she was sad that I had been so miserable. I felt better knowing that my mother knew and that I would not have to keep secrets from her. But I still worried about that big ugly spot in the middle of the carpet.

Then one day my mother brought home a very special machine. It was a carpet cleaning machine. It had a tank on it that put a cleaning fluid way down into the bottom of the carpet and pushed the dirt up into another tank.

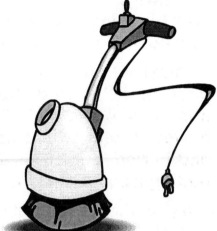

We carefully moved the furniture and took up the rug. The machine was very heavy and hard to handle, but, working together, my mom and I took it into the parlor and plugged it in. It made loud, gurgling noises that frightened me at first, but when we ran it over the muddy spot, I could see some of the dirt going up into the machine. Yes, the spot was definitely going away!

Questions/Activities

1. This story is about sexual abuse, but it has been interpreted quite differently by one group of individuals. This was a group of young adults in hospital treatment for chemical dependency. Can you guess what they saw as the girl's problem?

 Answer: That the girl had been using drugs or alcohol.

2. Why was the girl afraid to tell her mother about the spot on the carpet?

 Answer: There are possibly three reasons.
 A. She was afraid that her mother perhaps would not believe her about how the carpet got soiled.
 B. She was afraid that her mother, in not believing her, would not protect her and the carpet from another "attack."
 C. She was very much afraid that her mother would be angry at her.

 All of these are real concerns with childhood sexual abuse.

3. Why did the girl feel so bad when others admired the carpet?

Answer: Because she knew about the spot and felt like she was living a lie every time they admired the carpet.

4. When the girl thought about the carpet at school, she fell behind in her school work. What would happen if this continued?

Answer: She would begin to fail in school. This would create a serious problem, certainly involving her mother, her teacher and her principal. This would also affect her ability to handle frustration, making her very sensitive about everything.

5. What might happen next?

Answer: She would have difficulty with her behavior, moods and attitudes. Teachers might say that she didn't care, and she would have difficulty getting along with others, even her friends. She would have little motivation for doing much of anything.

6. What do they call these kinds of behaviors, moods and attitudes?

Answer: For starters, how about anger, sadness and anxiety?

7. What happens when people keep secrets about things they should tell someone about?

Answer: They can become anxious, depressed and sick.

8. Do you think that there is always a "machine" that will remove the problems in our lives?

Answer: Not really. Some consequences, whether they are our fault or not, are pretty permanent.

9. What can we do about those kinds of problems?

Answer: We can try to do the right thing, and we can look for some help from others. Sometimes we can only accept that damage has happened, and work at not letting it cripple our ability to live as honestly and as happily as possible.

10. Activity: "What is the Difference?"
Divide the group. Have them answer this question:

This story points to the difference between guilt and shame. What is the difference?

Answer: Guilt is a state of behavior; shame is a state of being. In the story, the girl was ashamed of the carpet, even though she was not the one who soiled it.

11. Can guilt and shame go together?

Answer: They usually do. A small child crawls up on the kitchen cabinet and reaches into the cookie jar just as his mother catches him. Obviously the child is guilty of trying to take a cookie without permission (guilt), and he knows he was disobedient (shame).

12. Can one be guilty without being ashamed?

Answer: Yes, especially if a person understands that what they are doing will serve a higher purpose, such as survival or protection of others.

13. Activity: "Guilt without Shame"
Divide the group into smaller groups. Have them answer this question and share it:
Can you think of any examples of guilt without shame?

Answer: A mother or father would steal food if they had to in order to feed their starving family. They would be guilty of stealing, but they would not consider themselves to be thieves because of the circumstances. As another example, any soldier who has gone to war understands that, in a battle, they might have to shoot and even kill one of the enemy. But they would not consider themselves to be a murderer.

14. Which one, guilt or shame, is more difficult to deal with?

Answer: Shame is always more difficult, as it involves negative decisions that one makes about themselves. Even though these decisions might be wrong and unhealthy, the person can be crippled by them for a lifetime.

Reference:

"The Carpet in My Parlor" was included in the original *Windows*.

The Journey

Application

This story explains how a certain amount of suffering might be necessary if an individual is to reach recovery (heal and regain functionality back in their lives). It is most useful to those who feel that they are through dealing with painful issues when they are not.

Prologue

"Dilley 9," the sign read. I had traveled that stretch of backroads hundreds of times as a consultant to the drug and alcohol treatment program at an out-of-the-way hospital in the small Texas town.

A thought struck me. How anxious would I have been to get to Dilley if, during the next nine miles, I was to encounter an economy-sized dose of inconvenience and hardship. Pictures of having six flat tires, vapor lock, brake failure and wearing Farmer Brown's best bull as a hood ornament came to view. Had those things happened, I would have arrived at the hospital a candidate for a bed myself.

What if I *knew* all that stuff was going to happen to me? Would I still make the trip? A good question. The answer would depend on my expectations of the destination. If I had a burning desire to get there, circumstances might slow me down, but they wouldn't stop me.

This story addresses through metaphor the willingness of one to experience pain and endure suffering in order to reach a valued and worthy goal. In the story *Recovery* is the destination; *Surrender* is the process of turning loose of self-will. *Denial* is the process of believing and acting as if problems do not exist, and *Minimization* is the process of underestimating the power and importance of existing problems.

The Story (The Journey)

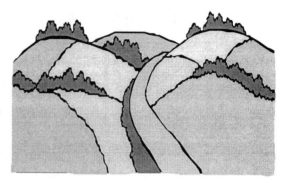

A motorist was on a long journey. He was hot, tired and *lost*. As he drove into a small town, he saw a farmer on the side of the road.

"Can you tell me the name of this town, Sir?" he asked.

"This is Minimization," the old fellow replied. "Where are you headed?"

"I've been trying to get to Recovery. It's been a long, hot drive, and I'm afraid I'm lost."

"Oh, Recovery. It's just straight down the road. Follow your nose for 20 more miles or so. You'll get there.

"Any other other towns on the way?" the traveler asked.

"Just a little place called Surrender," the farmer said, mopping at his brow with a large bandanna. "I reckon it's about 5 or 6 miles out of town."

"Anything between Surrender and Recovery?"

"Just a valley, the Valley of Legitimate Suffering."

"Is there a way to get to Recovery without going through the valley?" asked the motorist.

"Nope."

"Well, what if I just take a right up there at the traffic light?" the traveler questioned, pointing toward the intersection.

The farmer replaced his straw hat. "That turn will take you to the twin cities of Self-Pity and Resentment."

"How far?"

"Don't rightly know; never been there. But I've been told the trip can take a lifetime.

The traveler was concerned. "I'm not sure I like *any* of those choices. Is there some place where I can go to just think it all over?"

"You can go right back up the road you came in on. Stop at the first town you come to."

"And what town would that be?"

"That, sir," replied the farmer, "will be the city of Denial."

Questions/Activities

1. Activity: Terms

Either define these terms to the group, or let them define what they think they mean:

> **Minimization**
> **Recovery**
> **Surrender**
> **Legitimate Suffering**
> **Self-Pity**
> **Resentment**
> **Denial**

Answer: These definitions are given as they apply to the notion of recovery from feelings or behaviors that might hold us captive.

> A. **Minimization:** The process of making light of a problem or consequence.
> B. **Recovery:** The often painful realization that one's willpower and pride alone cannot "fix" the problem, compulsion or defect. Recovery includes the recognition of the destructive power of negative forces (including one's own thinking) and the willingness to accept the help of others.
> C. **Legitimate Suffering:** The sort of pain one willingly experiences in order to achieve healing. It is "legitimate" in the sense that it helps bring

closure to issues and an end to ongoing resentment. The process of legitimate suffering is sometimes called "getting real."

D. **Self-Pity:** The self-directed focus on hurts and wrongs that one elects to hold onto as a way of justifying one's inappropriate attitudes and behaviors. In a sense it is "illegitimate" suffering.

E. **Resentment:** Anger regarding specific hurts or injustices that has been cultivated to the point of producing destructive, poisonous seed. Resentment does not close; it just keeps going on. In fact, the word actually means to "re-feel."

F. **Denial:** The firm refusal to accept the notion that a compulsion, problem or defect exists, even when it is plainly obvious to others.

2. Activity: Rewriting

Break the group into a couple or three smaller groups. Have each group rewrite the story, but putting in the meanings of the words *Minimization, Recovery, Surrender, Legitimate Suffering, Self-Pity, Resentment* and *Denial* instead of the words themselves.

Answer: Here's a sample from part of the story:

"Can you tell me the name of this town, sir?" the traveler asked.

"Why, this is the place where folks always make light of their problems and circumstances," the old fellow replied. "Where are you headed?"

"I'm trying to get to that place where I have dealt as best I can with my problems and defects. I have been on a long drive, and I am lost."

3. The motorist in this story was told that he had to do two things in order to reach Recovery. What were they?

Answer: He had to surrender, and he had to be willing to do some appropriate, "legitimate" suffering. (This could bring up the subject of "illegitimate" suffering. This sort of suffering would produce an inappropriate benefit that prevents recovery. Choosing to hang onto anger and misery rather than considering forgiveness, or soaking in the pity that suffering might bring would be two examples.)

4. What are some examples of things that could happen to a person that would cause them to need Recovery?

Answer: All kinds of abuse and rejection, a severe problem with drugs and alcohol or a loss that is difficult to bear.

5. Are there really any shortcuts to Recovery?

Answer: No really, although folks might differ in the ways they surrender and suffer.

6. Then why do so many people search for an easier, softer way to get to Recovery?

Answer: Because they do not want to experience any pain at all. By the way, this is impossible.

7. What happens then?

Answer: They don't recover, which means that they keep experiencing resentment over and over again. Often their solution is to avoid pain by running away from problems and confrontations, or perhaps by numbing out their problems by synthetically altering their mood and feelings with drugs and alcohol.

8. Write the moral of this story. Be brief; don't use over two or three sentences.

Answer: For individuals to feel happy and fulfilled in life, they must be able to recognize problems and concerns that trouble them. They heal best when they let others help them, and when they realize that some degree of pain and discomfort are inescapable.

9. If you are working with a rather creative group, challenge them to discover another way to express the concept of recovery using a different kind of story.

Reference:

"The Journey" was part of the original *Windows*.

It Starts with an Apology

Application

This section addresses the "why, when and how" of making a sincere apology when one's actions have offended others.

Prologue

A heartfelt "I am sorry" cleanses. Everyone benefits, especially the person saying it. A genuine apology has a way of putting a relationship back on course again. And yet some folks rarely ever apologize for anything. Even though their behavior is far from perfect, it's as if an "I'm sorry" is beyond their ability to express. Why is that? Does it say deeper things about the person?

At the other extreme there are folks who can say "I'm sorry" a million times a day and never really mean it. It's almost as if their apologies are more like a form of manipulation.

I have a pet peeve. A lazy, ignorant or manipulative apology is much worse than none at all. A person who apologizes should know why they are apologizing. It makes sense the two would go together, but it doesn't always work out that way. For instance, we had a 4-year-old in our neighborhood who was taking mail out of the mailboxes on the street. His father rounded up his son's stash of folks' mail and took the little fellow house-to-house to give it back.

Standing on my porch, the boy said, "I'm sorry." I asked him what he was sorry for—and he just stared at me. He didn't have an answer because he didn't have a clue. The apology served no purpose at all. It was wasted.

The best apologies have feet; they move one to do as much as possible to make things right. A man I know tells that he was once so broke that he lied to a couple of Girl Scouts who came to his door selling cookies.

"Oh, I have *lots* of Girl Scout cookies in the house right now," he said. He began to feel terrible as he watched them leave. And he made himself a promise that he would never lie like that again. Some time later, he encountered some other Girl Scouts at his door. This time he was ready.

He listened politely to their pitch, then bought every box of cookies they had. As the girls were leaving, one of them turned toward him and said, "Mister, you're sure special."

He didn't have an opportunity to apologize to the girls he had lied to, but he had a change of heart and acted on it. And he was affirmed for it. What price some people would pay to hear *anyone* say to them: "You're sure special."

The following story explains how we should put more than words behind "I'm sorry." It was written by Zig Ziglar, professional speaker and best-selling author.

The Story (It Starts with an Apology)

I was raised during the Depression by a widowed mother with six children too young to work. Things were tough financially. Each one of us did what we could to make our contribution. Five milk cows, some fruit trees and a large garden provided most of our food. My brothers and I all got part-time jobs in a grocery store. My sisters worked in small department stores.

One of my responsibilities each morning was to take the cows out and stake them in good grass. At lunchtime, I would move them to another spot where there was more good grass.

One day, I was anxious to get back to school and play a little softball before the lunch break ended. In my hurry, I improperly staked one of the cows. She got loose and invaded a nearby garden.

125

That afternoon, when I returned for the cow, I was confronted by a lady who was upset because of what our cow had done to her garden. I apologized profusely, promised to be more careful in the future, and headed for home.

When Mom asked what had taken me so long, I told her what had happened. I recounted my apology and my mother said to me, "Son, to apologize is one thing, but to pay for what you did is more important." We returned to the lady to make restitution.

She estimated that the cow had eaten about eight bunches of turnip greens, valued at five cents a bunch, for a total of 40 cents. My mother paid the 40 cents.

That kind of money, 40 cents, doesn't sound like much money today, but in my grocery story job I earned five cents an hour, so forty cents represented eight hours of work. After that experience, when I staked the cows, they were well-staked. I believe that's one of the most important lessons I ever learned.

Questions/Activities

1. If young Ziglar's mother paid the 40 cents, why was he so careful to explain how long he had to work for that kind of money?

Answer: His mom might have paid the debt, but Zig had to work to pay back his mom. He had eight hours to think about how he would stake that cow next time.

2. His mother did not have to tell him to apologize for the damage the cow had done. Why?

Answer: Because he had already apologized to the lady before he told his mom about it. When he apologized, he also told the lady that he would be more careful next time. His mother knew the apology was genuine.

3. Does an apology always fix everything?

Answer: No; that's the point of this story. Whenever possible, we combine our apologies with an attempt to make restitution. Of course, there are those mistakes that cannot be fixed later. The best we offer is a heartfelt apology.

4. There's an old saying that goes: "Confession is good for the soul." An apology is sort of like a confession. What does "good for the soul" mean?

Answer: It means that if a person needs to apologize and doesn't, they will not feel right about it (maybe for a long, long time). Anytime we make an effort to do the right thing, especially when it is difficult, we will feel better about it.

5. Sometimes there are those people who apologize all the time, then keep on making the exact same mistakes. What about their apologies?

Answer: Maybe their apologies are not real. They could be a form of manipulation, or the sign of a person who might mean to change, but had great difficulty changing. With some people the apologies might be real when they say them, but they can't keep their promises. They might need to do more than apologize; they might need professional help.

6. Activity: Anatomy of an Apology

This is a group activity. Using this story and the experiences of the group, list the most important parts or characteristics of a sincere, heartfelt apology.

Answer: A few suggestions are listed below.
A. It must come from a contrite spirit (the person apologizing must feel bad about what they have done).
B. It must be specific.
C. It must indicate that the person apologizing will make an effort not to do it again (a kind of promise).
D. Whenever possible, the person needs to try to fix the problem.
E. It must offer the one wronged the choice of accepting or rejecting our apology.

Reference:

Zig Ziglar's story, "It Starts with an Apology," was printed in the fall, 1996, edition of my newsletter, *Reaching Out* (Vol. VIII, No. 1). It is reprinted here with his kind permission.

Charles

Application

This story addresses the ability for a person to genuinely exercise self-acceptance and self-forgiveness. In accomplishing this, the story also addresses issues of loss and anger.

Prologue

John Bradshaw, who for years operated a center for recovering families in Houston, is a global expert on the nature, effects and costs of addiction. He once said that, in his opinion, most emotional turmoil and mental illness is about unforgiveness.

There is the obvious issue of unforgiveness of others. There are those who choose to remain resentful and insulated in their anger than risk any vulnerability that forgiveness might bring. Such a position might produce short-term benefit, but the long-term picture is a miserable one. Have you ever known someone who was always angry (and probably scared, too)? These are not folks you want to be around for long.

At a much deeper level, forgiveness of self is more critical than forgiveness of others. Those who cannot forgive themselves are their own judge, jury and executioner. How do we know? Simple; they relegate their lives to the trash heap and make sure they stay there.

Unforgiveness of self is the mainspring that powers conditions like alcoholism, drug addiction and other compulsive disorders.

Charles' story is real indeed. He was one of the most decent and sensitive individuals I have ever known, but I could not convince him that he had those qualities.

He had to do that for himself.

The Story (Charles)

Charles and I were, without question, as different as two people could possibly be. I was a white, rural, middle-class professional; he was an inner city black, surviving only on welfare. Charles had come 2500 miles to do his best to break the clutches of alcohol and cocaine.

I was his doctor, the psychologist for the treatment center. My job was first to interview Charles. Fear and apprehension were etched into the premature lines across his face, but deep into his eyes there rested a gentleness, something marvelously serene. It was an element of certain hope that layered itself just behind a mask of incredible toughness.

The mask had served him well. It got him through prison and a hitch in Vietnam. The order for a marine was clear: either kill or be killed. So Charles killed plenty, and he stood helplessly by, consumed with rage, as he watched friends die and the body bags accumulate into piles.

But in war no one stops to mourn or grieve. You just go on. Besides, opium was cheap there. Enough of it blanketed all the feelings into numbness.

In treatment, Charles learned that drug and alcohol addiction flourished and thrives on toughness and numbness. The name of the game was simple: change or die.

Charles shared that he wanted to live, so he took a risk. He made a commitment to follow directions, even when those directions caused him to walk the paths of his greatest fears and pain.

One of his directions involved a mock funeral—the burial of the Vietnam experiences as Charles had lived them. It was a time of grieving and tears as Charles wrote of those times, name by name, face by face. With the support of his counselors and the other patients, Charles dug a hole and lovingly buried what he had recorded. He then stood, took three steps back and saluted the grave and the memories.

The toughness and the numbness were gone. Charles was becoming real. At last, he had found the road that leads to recovery.

Shortly after Charles had returned home, I was flipping through his chart. His handwritten comments on a piece of yellow legal pad caught my eye. It was his response to a direction to write how his epitaph would read. (This activity is a common direction given to patients in treatment. The activity often gives clues to a patient's deepest feelings about their future and their newfound sobriety.) What Charles shared was as unique as it was sensitive. In it, he demonstrated the ability to love others, for he was finally capable of loving himself. Charles' epitaph read:

> *Here rest the weary bones of one of God's chosen, for he was a martyr that stood amongst the righteous. His perseverance and valor shall be recorded in the annals of history. Now his spirit stands with the angels. Let the light of his memory shine forth as a beacon, a witness to all mankind.*

If you were to ask Charles about his recovery from drugs and alcohol, he would tell you that his sobriety is a gift that is handed to him in daily measure by a gracious and loving God. He would also tell you that sobriety is never a destination, but rather the journey.

———————————

Questions/Activities

1. Exactly what sort of things caused Charles to seek out opium when he was a marine in Vietnam?

Answer: It was mostly feelings that he could not handle at the time. The story mentions feelings about killing, the fear of being killed at any time and the feelings of watching friends die.

2. Exactly what is opium?

Answer: It's not that common in the United States, but it is a drug classed as an opioid. It is highly addictive and quite illegal on the street. Its effects on humans are very similar to heroin and morphine, which are also opioids. These drugs remove the sensation of pain without taking away consciousness and awareness (which is why soldiers,sailors and marines in combat situations carry morphine in their first-aid kits). Different types of opioids in the form of medications, patches and intravenous "drips" are administered to terminally ill cancer patients to help ease pain and suffering.

3. Did the opium (and the alcohol and cocaine) help Charles?

Answer: It helped for awhile. It threw a blanket over his pain and feelings that might have helped him through the moment. But covering feelings is not the same as dealing with them. Sooner or later, the pain and feelings work their way up, choking out healthy growth in the process. The price can be a dear one.

4. What did it cost Charles?

Answer: The story mentions drug and alcohol addiction, plus the fact that Charles could not work or hold down a job. He was on welfare when he came to treatment. He had also been in trouble with the law and had been in prison, all drug related. To Charles, however, the highest cost was his loss of self-respect.

5. Did other Vietnam veterans have these problems? Is something being done about it?

Answer: Yes, many had trouble. Today we call it Post Traumatic Stress Disorder or Delayed Post Traumatic Stress Disorder. But it wasn't just Vietnam veterans who have experienced it. With World War I veterans, we called it "Shell Shock," and with World War II and Korean War veterans we called it "Battle Fatigue." Today, more is being done to help veterans with these symptoms.

6. Why did Charles decide to follow directions in treatment?

Answer: He was finally willing to trust those who gave the directions. Charles had learned that, as long as he was in control, he would only get sicker (and probably die).

7. Is it hard to give up that kind of control?

Answer: It is so hard that many choose to die instead. These are the ones who, to the very end, will convince themselves they either have no problems or that they do not need any help with them.

8. Did the mock funeral really make a difference to Charles? Why?

Answer: Yes, because it allowed him to close a painful part of his past by deciding to deal with it all just one more time—appropriately. It allowed him, with the support of others, to feel whatever he needed to feel. In treatment this is called "getting real."

9. What did Charles' epitaph say about him?

Answer: It said that he had learned to accept, love and serve others because he had finally learned to accept and love himself.

10. But might some folks think that Charles' epitaph is conceited and self-serving?

Answer: A good question. Consider the directions he was given. Rather than being directed to write his epitaph, Charles was directed to share how his epitaph would read. This means it could have been written by others (friends or family). In essence, the direction encouraged Charles to take a look at how *others* would remember him.

11. This story also shows that Charles was finally able to forgive himself for all the mistakes he had made. How important is forgiveness of self and others?

Answer: It's critical to healing, but be clear that the only one who can decide to forgive is the one who has been wronged. Forgiveness cannot be ordered or mandated.

12. Is it okay, then, to try to forgive those who have wronged you or hurt you in some way?

Answer: It's certainly okay to want to forgive them, especially if forgiveness is being sought. Sometimes folks attempt to forgive someone who denies that they have ever done anything wrong. This can create tremendous problems in relationships. In situations like this, a conscious willingness to forgive someone, if and when they ever ask, can help a person deal with the problem in the relationship and get on with their life. This is called the "spirit" of forgiveness (as it would differ from an "act" of forgiveness).

13. Is Charles cured now?

Answer: In his recovery, Charles would be the first to remind us that no former addict or alcoholic is ever really "cured." But Charles *is* set free from the bonds of his addiction. Sobriety and functional living come only in *daily* doses.

14. Activity: Your Epitaph

Answer: Encourage the members of your group to have a vision of what their epitaph (tombstone) will say 200 years from now. (Again, emphasize how it would read, not how *they* would write it.) Share these.

Reference:

The story, "Charles," appeared in the original *Windows*.

'Til Joy Comes Back

Application

This story shows how activity (just about any activity) and a willingness to follow a few simple directions can be helpful to a person experiencing emotional distress.

Prologue

Self-doubt, insecurity, depression and many forms of mental distress incubate best in a state of inactivity. Ask a distressed person what they feel like doing, and they will quickly tell you, "Nothing!" As one comes to a standstill, deeper go self-doubt, insecurity and depression.

Although meaningful and productive work is not the answer for every problem in life, it at least defeats inactivity. Work encourages one to "do" something, and that's generally good. (It would not be good if the point of work is to avoid ever dealing with with difficult problems and issues.)

Here's a poem I found tacked on the wall at a car dealership in my hometown. It's simply titled, *"Work."*

> If you are poor, **work**.
>
> If you are rich, continue to **work**.
>
> If you are happy, keep right on **working**.
>
> If disappointments come, **work**.
>
> If sorrow overwhelms you, and loved ones seem not true, **work**.
>
> When faith falters, **work**
>
> When dreams are shattered and hope seems dead, **work**.
>
> Whatever happens or matters, **work**.

__Work__ faithfully, __work__ with faith.

__Work__ is the greatest material remedy available.

__Work__ will cure many mental and physical afflictions.

It's pretty difficult to overstate the simple philosophy here. Although activity is not the one-dose cure for every problem, it's not a bad place to start. I've worked with youngsters who were bogged down in inertia and have asked them to do something that requires them to follow directions and put out a little effort (such as taking a lap around the track or playground before going home after school). Their responses to the suggestion can say a lot about their healing. If they argue about it, posing questions of what good it would do, a long journey remains. Their own thinking and desire to anticipate and control all outcomes are holding them back. Generally, they will remain "stuck" and unhappy longer than necessary.

If, on the other hand, a youngster trusts you well enough to do what you ask, they will, at the very least, follow directions. Additionally, the activity almost always does some good that even the youngster can recognize. And, as a bonus, trust deepens.

The Story ('Til Joy Comes Back)

I was wrapping up a day of seeing children at a group home in south Texas (one of my favorite "retreats"; these kids and the adults who serve them are *my* therapy). I walked over to the administration building to drop off some dictation. A girl was sweeping acorns off the sidewalk; I'll call her Suzy.

I already knew she had been suspended from school that day for starting a fight. Joy, her caseworker, picked her up from school and brought her back to the facility. As a consequence (it is very important that a youngster realize that coming home under these circumstances will not be a positive event), Joy gave the girl a broom and the task of sweeping acorns off the sidewalk. She had an appointment for a meeting at one of the cottages, but carefully instructed Suzy to keep on working until she returned.

I guess I felt a little sorry for her; it was getting pretty late. I asked Suzy how much longer she was supposed to keep working. Her reply spoke volumes:

"Til Joy comes back."

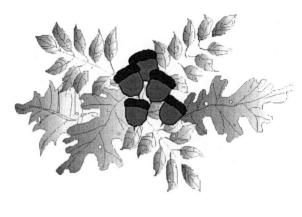

Questions/Activities

1. This is a very short story, but what does it tell us about Suzy?

Answer: First of all, she is living in a group home with other children. This means that she can't live at home with her family, although we don't really know why. The story also says that Suzy was sent home because she was fighting at school. Maybe it's possible she had trouble with her temper (and that might have something to do with her family situation).

2. "Til Joy comes back" can mean a couple of things. Explain.

Answer: It could mean that she is supposed to do what Joy told her to do, and that she would be in more trouble if she quit before Joy came back. It could also mean that, just perhaps, sweeping acorns off the sidewalk gives her time to calm down and think about what she could do to be happier and stay out of trouble. And, if she does a good job with the sidewalk, she might be joyful about it. If Joy later told Suzy that she did a good job, that would help, too.

3. Can these meanings be helpful to someone like Suzy?

Answer: Of course.

4. Have you ever known you should do something, but felt too sad or too upset to do it? How did you feel about it?

Answer: Sure, we all have felt this way at some time. If we know we should do something, and don't do it, we usually feel even worse.

5. Did you ever make yourself do it anyway? How did you feel then?

Answer: Usually you felt a little better. That's what this story is about.

6. Do we always know what we should do whenever we feel sad or upset? What if someone we trust and respect makes a suggestion?

Answer: No, we don't, but we might think we do. If someone we trust and respect makes a suggestion about what we could do, we should consider doing it.

7. What if we do what they suggest, but it doesn't fix everything? Does that mean that it was a bad idea?

Answer: Of course not. If they care about you, and they thought what they asked you to do was a good idea, you might benefit even if it didn't fix everything. For certain, you did *something*, and you followed their directions. That's a good start. It shows them you value them and their desire to help you.

8. Would doing some kind of work when you feel sad or upset ever be the wrong thing to do?

Answer: It could be the wrong thing to do if a person was working instead of ever dealing with their feelings. Working as a way of avoiding relationships or having to deal with problems is called a "defocus." If it is a persistent and serious problem, it's a form of compulsive behavior (addiction) we call "workaholism."

Reference:

The poem, "Work," is from *The Silent Partner*. I could identify no further reference.

The One That Got Away

Application

This story speaks to the hopelessness and despair of addiction—and the joy of overcoming it.

Prologue

Even young children know that the misuse and abuse of drugs and alcohol can be devastating. But unfortunately knowledge does not solve the problem. Addiction continues to wreak havoc and death in the lives of those who are well aware of its destructiveness.

This story offers a first person "window" that not only shows the pain of addiction, but of the victory of recovery. The story took place in a hospital, a drug treatment program. The young man who wrote it was my patient, a young adult in his early 20s. I'll call him Chris.

Chris was absolutely and totally addicted to crack cocaine. When I first saw him in the hospital, cocaine had cost him his family, his job, his self-respect and nearly his life. Fortunately, his desire for recovery was strong. As a part of his treatment, Chris was instructed to write a letter to the addiction that had so consumed him. He gave me permission to share it with others. It's a powerful letter. Whenever I share it with a group of educators or young people, it never fails to touch the hearts of those who hear it.

The Story (A Letter to Cocaine)

I got to know you when I was very young. You were kind to me. You eased the pain. You helped me to forget. When I was having trouble in social situations, you gave me the courage to speak up. For years you helped me to accept others and to be accepted.

I trusted you and loved you, and I knew that you loved me, too. When I had given myself totally to you, you pounced on me like the blood-sucking viper you really are. You drained me slowly and cruelly of life, gripping me like a vice around my throat. When you had filled yourself, robbing me of all my emotions, you were not satisfied. You wanted all of me, and slowly you began to consume me. Ever so slowly, while I watched helplessly, you took me, your black eyes shining with delight as I trembled.

But you took too long. You took your own sweet time, toying with me 'til you let me get away. With the help of God and some beautiful people, I slipped out of your sewer of a mouth. How does it feel to die? How does it feel to die slowly? Get used to it, 'cause you ain't gonna feed off me no more.

I'm the one who's smiling now. I'm the one with the shining eyes. Now you live with the pain; you live with the nightmares. I'll live knowing that you suffer, and I plan on living a long, long time. Rot slowly ... burn slowly ... starve slowly.

Signed—*The One That Got Away*

Questions/Activities

1. This is an angry letter. Is it right for someone to be this upset?

Answer: Anger is not a bad emotion. In fact, anger is energy and direction that can help a person deal effectively with a problem (of course, used inappropriately, the same anger can also destroy a person). Chris was angry that he was deceived (almost to the point of death).

2. At some point didn't Chris know that his use of cocaine was costing him a great deal?

Answer: Perhaps, but by then it was almost too late.

3. Why didn't he just stop using cocaine?

Answer: Because Chris was one of those persons who couldn't stop on his own. That's the nature of addiction. He really didn't want to go to the hospital either, but he was too sick to offer much resistance.

4. But I've heard people say that someone can stop abusing alcohol and drugs if they really want to. Isn't that true?

Answer: Sometimes; there are those folks who can put it down and be done with it. But there aren't many who can do that. Take a look; if a person is saying that they can quit anytime they want to, but everything in their life is falling completely to pieces, there's a serious problem. Addiction is a disease. That's why it's treated in hospitals and covered under insurance. You don't cure a disease by really wanting it to go away. It's the same with addiction.

5. Are there other kinds of addiction?

Answer: Addiction is addiction, but people can be addicted to anything that is mood-altering: drugs, alcohol, food, gambling, sex, entertainment, all kinds of things.

6. Can people be addicted to other people?

Answer: Certainly. Addiction to people is called "enmeshment." It occurs when a person latches onto another person as a way of making themselves feel better. We all occasionally need soothing and reassurance from others, but if we must have it all the time, that's addiction. Strong and healthy people have the ability to soothe and reassure themselves when the going gets tough.

7. Activity: Letter to Chris

Encourage the youngsters to write a letter of encouragement to Chris. Let them share their letters with the group.

Alphabetical Reference: Topic to Story

Notes

Notes